Paradise In The Waste Land

Early Works

T.S. Eliot

Critical Introduction by
Jeremiah Webster

Wiseblood Classics Volume XVII

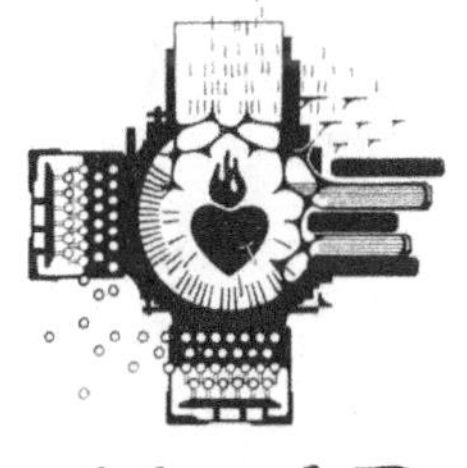

Wiseblood Books

Milwaukee, Wisconsin

Wiseblood Books

www.wisebloodbooks.com

Cover Image: Ruins of a church in Gary, Indiana

Library of Congress Cataloging-in-Publication Data

Eliot, T.S., 1888-1965

Paradise in The Waste Land: poetry, stories, essays/ T.S. Eliot;

1. Eliot, T.S., 1888-1965—poetry, stories, essays
2. Modernism 3. Religion and Literature
4. Philosophy and Poetry
5. Jeremiah Webster

ISBN-13: 978-0615914626

ISBN-10: 0615914624

TABLE OF CONTENTS

The inhabited cities shall be laid waste, and the land shall become a desolation; and you shall know that I am the Lord.

- Ezekiel 12:20

Modern Mandrake:
Reviving the Poetry of T.S. Eliot

If Madame Sosostris shuffled her "wicked pack of cards"[1] today, would she find the hanged man, the lady of situations, the great wheel? Would Stetson walk among the dead? Would Cleopatra reign from a gilded throne? Would the virtues (*Datta, Dayadhvam, Damyata*) offer new promise, or would April prove equally cruel, beyond all hope of spring? We are ninety one years removed from *The Waste Land* (1922). T.S. Eliot's poem is now older than The Great Depression, the atomic bomb, Bob Dylan, DOS, and the ubiquitous smartphone.

In spite of its age, the poem is a remarkably contemporary metaphor. Detroit and the Rust Belt's decaying infrastructure are easy substitutes for the Unreal City.[2] "Shall I at least set my lands in order,"[3] no longer Isaiah's utterance in the face of mortality, is now the ironic ethos of a cloistered suburbia. The tone deafness of American politics, of religious *ressentiment*, mirrors the landscape of "no water but only rock / Rock and no water and the sandy road."[4] The fear Eliot promised "in a handful of dust"[5] still has teeth in an age of banker bailouts and interminable war. If anything, Goldman Sachs makes Jay Gatsby look quaint, provincial in his Jazz Age decadence. Tired of bootlegging? Try credit default swaps and derivatives.

---

[1] *The Waste Land* ln. 46

[2] Ibid. ln. 60

[3] Ibid. ln. 425

[4] Ibid. ln. 331-32

[5] Ibid. ln. 30

For a surplus of reasons, Eliot's poetry deserves a new readership. As the United States continues to seek departed nymphs through the incantations of technology, as moral impotence becomes the norm, the jeremiad voice of *The Waste Land* is a much needed corrective; its pessimism may in fact be the best prescription for our time. Eliot's critique of Victorian decay, of the bankruptcy of empire, "Falling towers / Jerusalem Athens Alexandria / Vienna London / Unreal,"[6] is a necessary rejoinder for a generation still trying to maintain a Post-WWII "American Dream." As prosperity becomes increasingly mirage-like in the Twenty First Century, as decadence begets debt, as *shalom* is pursued through duplicitous governance and predator drones, the poem's final lamentation, "Shantih, Shantih, Shantih,"[7] is an apt benediction for our age. To survey this "heap of broken images"[8] as Eliot so courageously does, is to recognize that all is not well, that unless there is revelation, "the sound of water over a rock,"[9] unless we are able to answer, "Who is the third who walks always beside you?,"[10] there is little reason for hope.

After the torchlight red on sweaty faces
After the frosty silence in the gardens
After the agony in stony places
The shouting and the crying
Prison and palace and reverberation
Of thunder of spring over distant mountains
He who was living is now dead
We who were living are now dying
With a little patience.[11]

---

[6] Ibid. ln. 374-77
[7] Ibid. ln. 434
[8] Ibid. ln. 22
[9] Ibid. ln. 356-57
[10] Ibid. ln. 360
[11] Ibid. ln. 322-330

Eliot Among Moderns

Poets of the early Twentieth Century perceived a *sharp break from the past,* not just in their own lives, but within the larger gestalt as well. As Virginia Woolf wryly observed, " . . . on or about December 1910 human character changed."[12] Scholars date the shift even earlier, with Emily Dickinson and Walt Whitman serving as precursors to a Twentieth Century avant-garde. Modernism was a sea change, a new ordering of consciousness. When the Armory Show of Modern Art appeared in New York City (1913), few knew how to respond: what to make of Picasso's *Woman With Mustard Pot* (1910), Dasburg's *Lucifer* (1912), or Duchamp's *Nude Descending a Staircase* (1912). To cite Cole Porter, it was all so *everything goes.* One thing was clear: Victorian sensibilities were passé and a new aesthetic, one that would take nearly a hundred years for the public to embrace, was making forays in the visual and literary arts.

For Hugh Kenner, Ezra Pound catalyzed much of what was new, chic, and subversive about Modern poetry.[13] Pound was the scouting agent, promoting the careers of T.S. Eliot and H.D., William Carlos Williams and Gertrude Stein. The Imagist movement, of which Pound was an advocate, informed Eliot's objective correlative, Amy Lowell's exploration of Chinese linguistics, and (arguably) Wallace Stevens' distinction between a blue and a green world. The "Pound Era" is nearly impossible to summarize, so divergent are the aims of its practitioners. This is a literature as dismissive of past traditions as it is obsessed with them. Poems reference automobiles and Apollonian chariots, seek spiritual consolation as they spit on past altars, renovate the rules of syntax, and critique technopoly with footnotes from Homer,

---

[12] "Mr. Bennett and Mrs. Brown" - Virginia Woolf (1924)

[13] *The Pound Era* (1971)

Virgil, and Dante. Modernist poetry is multifaceted in both style and substance, an era fixated with time in perhaps the same way that Postmodernism is preoccupied with space, gender, identity, and race.

Such ambitions led to accusations of elitism. "T.S. Eliot never met an obscure reference he didn't like," one of my graduate school professors dismissively opined. John Crowe Ransom described the Moderns as poets who "could not have estranged the public more completely if they had tried."[14] Equally damning was the "problem of form"[15] cited by J.V. Cunninham and others, as though the break from traditional meter, from Nineteenth Century poesy, signaled a literary apocalypse. For the gatekeepers of tradition, Prometheus was unbound.

Poetic schools during the second half of the Twentieth Century attempted to distance themselves from Modernism. Confessional and Beat poets appear reactionary to the prerequisites Modern poetry placed on readers: encyclopedic breadth, linguistic aptitude, classical training, and a patience usually reserved for Wagner's *Der Ring des Nibelungen*. One could also argue that such demands single-handedly created the English professor / literary critic: a Tiresias in tweed, priest of the belletristic sacrament. Never before had a literature necessitated such a league of "experts." But the Modern embrace of the enigmatic, of *high* and *low* culture, resulted from an inability to escape the canon. Put succinctly, the era inspired the poets, not the other way around. These were writers who, having grown up under the banner of colonialism, now witnessed the consequences. Modern poets were keenly aware of the crisis of civilization and the casualties of world war.[16] Like Coleridge's Mariner, the poetry wore its own albatross, making the verse, and here I incite my own controversy, an intensely moral and prophetic endeavor. The Moderns would have dismissed this

---

[14] *The World's Body* (1938)

[15] *Praising it New* - Garrick Davis, Ed. (2008) pg. 221

[16] See the poems of Wilfred Owen

claim outright, but their work betrays a very real anxiety towards the recognized schism from moral objectivity and religious assurance that occurred in their lifetimes. Rather than merely subvert past conventions, Modern poetry searched for a viable worldview, fragmented yes, unencumbered by tradition to be sure, but *knowable*. It perceived the despairing "present" of the Twentieth Century and attempted to recast the world again.

Wallace Stevens' appraisal of "empty heaven and its hymns"[17] demanded an alternative.[18] W.B. Yeats' *The Second Coming* (1919) was a poem of terrible anticipation, awaiting a "rough beast" the next gyre would bring. Like its author, the poem genuinely expected revelation to participate in the modern outlook and aesthetic. Yeats' recognition that "Things fall apart; the centre cannot hold," was a vital first step in appraising an era where, "The falcon cannot hear the falconer."[19] One hears the rhetoric of the Hebrew prophets in Yeats and Eliot, Hopkins and Jeffers. Notice the *life in death* affirmation, the didactic voice *crying in the wilderness* that resides in Robinson Jeffers' poem *Shine, Perishing Republic*:

> While this America settles in the mould of its vulgarity,
> heavily thickening
> to empire,
> And protest, only a bubble in the molten mass, pops and
> sighs out, and the
> mass hardens.
>
> I sadly smiling remember that the flower fades to make fruit
> the fruit rots
> to make earth.

---

[17] *The Man With the Blue Guitar* (1937)

[18] See *Sunday Morning* (1915)

[19] Ibid. ln. 3, ln.2

Out of the mother: and through the spring exultances,
ripeness
and decadence; and home to the mother.

You making haste haste on decay: not blameworthy; life is good, be it
stubbornly long or suddenly
A mortal splendor: meteors are not needed less than mountains: shine,
perishing republic.

But as for my children, I would have them keep their
distance from the
thickening center; corruption
Never has been compulsory, when the cities lie at the monster's feet there
are left the mountains.

And boys, be in nothing so moderate as in love of man
a clever servant, insufferable master.
There is the trap that catches noblest spirits, that caught —they say—
God, when he walked on earth.[20]

Osiris would indeed rise again, but not in the way anyone expected, and certainly not through religion, that "old dispensation."[21] Writers tended to embrace Nietzsche's contention that Judaism and Christianity were resentful outgrowths of the

[20] *Shine, Perishing Republic – Tamar* (1917-23)
[21] *Journey of the Magi* (1927)

slave morality,[22] pursue art as an expression of Übermensch, or endorse a broad Whitmanesque form of humanism. T.S. Eliot's conversion to the Anglican church was a notable exception. The metaphysics of Modern poetry, and a shift towards intellectual materialism, alienated these writers even further from a culture more content to ask with ambivalence *Quid est veritas?* than to wrestle with the kind of doubt one finds as early as Tennyson.[23]

* * *

Just as it asked essential questions, Modern poetry embraced "the art of getting meaning into words."[24] This endeavor appeared in Formalist and New Critical approaches to literature. It was evident in the hermeneutics Pound and Eliot endorsed as proponents of Modernism. The critical work was prescriptive, with Pound devising precepts in "ABC of Reading" (1934) as New Critics like R.P. Warren, Yvor Winters, and Allen Tate offered astute, albeit formulaic, approaches to literature.[25] This resulted in a culture of rich artistic innovation and deep rumination.

But how do we conceptualize the relationship between history, past tradition, and Eliot's notion of the individual talent, Carl Sandberg's everyman politic, or Pound and James Joyce's re-imagining of Ulysses? Could one reconcile the Modern age with the metanarratives of the past? Clearly the Moderns were selective in their appropriations and abandonments. They chose their allegiances carefully. In T.S. Eliot, for example, we find an author who inhabited Pound's "Make it New" mantra while

---

[22] See *On the Genealogy of Morals* (1887)

[23] See *In Memoriam* – Canto 54-55 (1849)

[24] *Praising it New* - Garrick Davis, Ed. (2008) pg. 31

[25] "Pure and Impure Poetry"(1942) / "The Morality of Poetry"(1937) / "Is Literary Criticism Possible?" (1950)

simultaneously going about the business of canon preservation. Eliot held complementary, antagonistic, and ambivalent views towards history and the present. In his "Tradition and the Individual Talent" (1919), Eliot made the following assertion:

> No poet, no artist of any art, has his complete meaning alone. His significance, his appreciation is the appreciation of his relation to the dead poets and artists. You cannot value him alone; you must set him, for contrast and comparison, among the dead.[26]

In Eliot's case, "complete meaning" meant incorporating past works (Chaucer, Dante, Julian of Norwich, Shakespeare, Arnold, Tennyson, Baudelaire, etc.) into the aesthetic logic and cadence of his poetry. This created intrinsic difficulty, demanding much of the reader, but it was consistent with Eliot's view that "poets in our civilization, as it exists at present, must be difficult."[27] Poems like *The Waste Land* and *Four Quartets* (1943) are containers of culture, encyclopedic vessels of preservation. For Eliot, a wide and embracing gaze assisted meaning in an increasingly meaningless age, not the reverse.

Given this premise, readers are often startled by Eliot's conversion, and the influence of Christianity on his later work. Was not Christianity the great enemy of intellectual life, a barbarism best abandoned? Eliot's grappling with faith and doubt in a poem like *Ash Wednesday* (1930) was perceived as antithetical to the aims of the Modern project. Ironically, Eliot's Modernist ambitions genuinely led him to orthodoxy, where he perceived anew the elegance of a Christian conception of body and soul, sin and redemption. While his contemporaries balked,[28] Eliot

---

26 "Tradition and the Individual Talent" (1919)

27 "The Isolation of Modern Poetry" - *The Kenyon Review* Vol. 3, No. 2 (Spring 1941) pg. 209-220

28 In *The Cantos*, No. 29, Pound famously remarked, "But this beats me, / Beats me, I mean that I do not understand it; / This love of

confronted the alienation of the Twentieth Century with a renewed passion for the Christian Gospel, and the *wounded surgeon*, "Whose constant care is not to please / But to remind of our and Adam's curse, / And that, to be restored, our sickness must grow worse."[29] In a startling synthesis of both old and new, Eliot forged his own way through the waste land. His conversion to Anglicanism in 1927 was more radical than his contemporaries cared to admit. Eliot's embrace of tradition, of the *logos* of John's gospel, was its own progress. It was, by its very nature, a reaction to the status quo of secularism, decadence, and a political liberalism that attempted to fill the void of religious faith in modern society.

The enigma of Eliot, the gift of those latter-day poems,[30] is that Christian faith allowed him to reside in the complexities of human suffering and despair. It did not negate his commitment to intellectual life as the critics of Christianity often suggest.[31] Quite the opposite. *Four Quartets* conceptualizes God as " . . . the still point of the turning world,"[32] the fixed reference point by which one engages with the temporal. Readers are often surprised that the author of *The Waste Land* and *Four Quartets* is one and the same, but the ambitions of *Eliot Humanist* and *Eliot Christian* follow the same trajectory. Any meaningful vision of heaven begins with the pandemonium of hell. Like Dante's *The Divine Comedy*, Eliot's *The Waste Land* serves as *Inferno* to the *Purgatorio* (and intimation of *Paradiso*) one finds in *Four Quartets*. The desolation of *The Waste Land* is, in the words of the Eliot himself, "not a separation from belief; it is nothing so pleasant. In fact, doubt, uncertainty, futility etc., would seem to me to prove anything

---

death that is in them" in response to Eliot's convictions.

29 *Four Quartets - East Coker* ln. 154-56

30 See *Journey of the Magi / Ash Wednesday / A Song for Simeon / Four Quartets*

31 See the writings of Ludwig Feuerbach, Frederick Nietzsche, and Bertrand Russell respectively.

32 *Four Quartets - Burnt Norton* ln. 62

except this agreeable partition; for doubt and uncertainty are merely a variety of belief."[33] *The Waste Land* and *Four Quartets* are not separated by desolation and belief; we find nothing so pleasant. They are variations on a theme. The "pool among the rock"[34] returns as a pool "filled with water out of sunlight."[35] *The Waste Land's* suggestion of "death by water,"[36] and the "sound of water over a rock,"[37] is answered with fire in *Four Quartets*: "The only hope, or else despair / Lies in the choice of pyre or pyre – / To be redeemed from fire by fire."[38] The "one walking beside you,"[39] finds definition in "The hint half guessed at, the gift half understood . . . Incarnation."[40] Each of these moments advances a pilgrimage that seeks revelation outside of time and a Word beyond language. The journey readers experience from the despair of the Unreal City to the edenic reality of the Mystic Rose embodies the epigraph from Heraclitus,[41] and is beautifully summarized at the end of *Little Gidding*:

> We shall not cease from exploration
> And the end of all our exploring
> Will be to arrive where we started
> And know the place for the first time.[42]

---

[33] *T.S. Eliot: An Imperfect Life* - Lyndall Gordon (1999) pg. 189

[34] *The Waste Land* ln. 351

[35] *Four Quartets - Burnt Norton* ln. 35

[36] *The Waste Land* ln. 55

[37] *The Waste Land* ln. 355

[38] *Four Quartets - Little Gidding* ln. 205-6

[39] *The Waste Land* ln. 362

[40] *Four Quartets - The Dry Salvages* ln. 215

[41] *Four Quartets - Epigraph*: "The way up and the way down are one and the same."

[42] *Four Quartets - Little Gidding* ln. 239-42

For Eliot, to "arrive where we started" meant a return to the very faith modernity had abandoned. This makes Eliot a unique figure in Modern poetry, an artist who begins with the presuppositions of his peers but draws entirely different conclusions. As he writes in "Thoughts after Lambeth":

> The World is trying the experiment of attempting to form a civilized but non-Christian mentality. The experiment will fail; but we must be very patient in awaiting its collapse; meanwhile redeeming the time: so that the Faith may be preserved alive through the dark ages before us; to renew and rebuild civilization, and save the World from suicide.[43]

Just as Euripides "believed in a world he disliked,"[44] the Moderns were at odds with the tyranny of science and the empirical mechanisms of business and industry that acknowledged the body but denied the soul. Poetry was no longer considered essential for a citizenry of the factory, the stock market, or the skyscraper. Only a few of the poets surveyed in this essay received recognition in their lifetimes. Gertrude Stein's first novel, *Three Lives* (1909), sold but a few hundred copies. Ezra Pound's *The Cantos* (1915-1962), the *Ulysses* of poetry, was comfortable on doctoral bookshelves, but out of place in the home. Eliot, with his mermaids and coffee spoons, enjoyed some of the success the Fireside Poets had known during the Nineteenth Century, but the fundamental tenor of the Moderns was one of alienation. The works of Wallace Stevens and Mina Loy, among others, were never (in form or aspiration) the kind of "hearth and home reading" of a Longfellow, Bryant, or Whittier. As Delmore Schwartz describes it in his "The Isolation of Modern Poetry":

---

[43] "Thoughts after Lambeth" (1931)

[44] *Euripides I* - Richard Lattimore (1955) pg. vii

> On the one hand, there was no room in the increasing industrialization of society for such a monster as the cultivated man; a man's taste for literature had at best nothing to do with most of the activities which constituted daily life in an industrial society. On the other hand, culture, since it could not find a place in modern life, has fed upon itself increasingly and has created its own autonomous satisfactions, removing itself further all the time from any essential part in the organic life of society.[45]

Modern poets experienced a kind of *renaissance negativa*. A generation of remarkable innovation, intellect, and artistry was divorced from its own time and place; writers haunted by the past were abrogated in the present. Schwartz suggests that like the priest, the poet became "an essentially comic figure."[46] The modern poet, defrocked from the privileged status once enjoyed by Catullus, Horace, and Virgil, was reduced to a punch line, a parody. The overwhelming pragmatism of the Twentieth Century, the uncoupling of the modern mind from myth, the noise of industrial ambition, what George Steiner describes as "the systematic suppression of silence,"[47] made poetry the least envied of all professions. Here indeed was a generation, "Wandering between two worlds, one dead, / The other powerless to be born."[48] Like prophets, these writers gave utterance to humanitarian and spiritual decay as the world refashioned Gomorrah.

---

[45] "The Isolation of Modern Poetry" - *The Kenyon Review* Vol. 3, No. 2 (Spring 1941) pg. 209-220

[46] Ibid.

[47] *No Passion Spent: Essays 1978-1996* - George Steiner (2010) pg. xiii

[48] *Stanzas from the Grande Chartreuse* - Matthew Arnold (1855) ln. 85

The Moderns turned inward, a prelude to poetry's eventual residence in the academy. It was in this interior space that they found, thanks in large measure to the emerging field of psychology, a landscape as rich as the visions that had preoccupied much of poetry up to the Twentieth Century. They explored subjectivity in ways that Homer's hexameter or the terza rima of Dante could not. The degree to which each poet engaged with the influences of history was dependent on the ambition of their projects. That the range of approaches was so vast speaks well of the Moderns, a generation that witnessed revolution from all sides, and in many cases incited their own.

Reading Eliot

> For myself, I can only say that a knowledge of the springs that released a poem is not necessarily a help towards understanding the poem: too much information about the origins of the poem may even break my contact with it.[49]

Would the poet *par excellence* be appalled by an introduction such as this accompanying his work? Perhaps. And yet it was Eliot's own refusal to address inquiry and his notoriously aloof persona that encouraged the industry of Eliot Criticism Inc. While it has been popular to besmirch *Eliot the Conservative,*[50] *Eliot the Sexual Impotent,*[51] *Eliot the Anti-Semite,*[52] such possibilities often digress into *ad hominem* caricatures. The better point of inquiry is to begin with the work itself. It is here that Eliot reveals the most. The poems display a writer in pursuit of a comprehensive existence.

---

[49] "The Frontiers of Criticism" (1961)

[50] See "T.S. Eliot" - George Orwell - *Essays* (1968)

[51] See *Mr. and Mrs. Eliot* - Earnest Hemingway - *In Our Time* (1925)

[52] Craig Raine offers a compelling rebuttal to this common accusation in his *T.S. Eliot: Lives and Legacies* (2006)

For Eliot, emphasis on emotion alone (cue Romanticism) is a grotesque idolatry. Tedious pragmatism (cue Dryden) is equally narrow. Eliot seeks an emotional and intellectual "middle way," a holistic vision of humanity on equal footing with his mentor Dante. He may employ the fragment, but he's after the whole.

> Every phrase and every sentence is an end and a beginning,
> Every poem an epitaph. And any action
> Is a step to the block, to the fire, down the sea's throat
> Or to an illegible stone: and that is where we start.
> We die with the dying:
> See, they depart, and we go with them.
> We are born with the dead:
> See, they return, and bring us with them.
> The moment of the rose and the moment of the yew-tree
> Are of equal duration. A people without history
> Is not redeemed from time, for history is a pattern
> Of timeless moments. So, while the light fails
> On a winter's afternoon, in a secluded chapel
> History is now and England.[53]

* * *

So how do readers stay moored in poems that often provoke a bewildering sense of intellectual inadequacy? Where does one find the Eliot of deep feeling? How can we breathe a little life into seemingly inscrutable embers? A few observations:

---

[53] *Four Quartets - Little Gidding* ln. 224-37

(1) *These fragments I have shored against my ruins*

The fragmentary nature of Eliot's verse is a reliable pitfall. It helps to think of the poet *tuning in* to various broadcasts on a radio dial (a distinctly modern pastime), or the act of channel surfing which, by its very nature, is impossible to summarize cogently. *The Waste Land* is a cacophony of voices, with commentary from London's inhabitants, the hyacinth girl, Germanic nobility, Madame Sosostris, and a world of others. Eliot mimics the fractured linguistic of contemporary life. He anticipates the sound bite, the unavoidable eavesdropping one experiences in a world where one-sided cell phone conversations are the norm. One can only imagine the poetry Eliot would have devised with the parlance of texting or Facebook.

As with Robert Browning, the dramatic monologue is also essential in Eliot's verse. Eliot not only utilizes the monologue in the traditional sense–to reveal an interior self–but to suggest a collective consciousness as well. As with all fiction and poetry, it is a critical mistake to assume the "I" in Eliot's poetry is the author, or a reflection of his personal convictions. In fact, knowing exactly *who* says, "My nerves are bad tonight. Yes, bad. Stay with me,"[54] or "I think we are in rats' alley, / Where the dead men lost their bones,"[55] or, "To Carthage then I came / burning burning burning burning / O Lord Thou pluckest me / O Lord Thou pluckest / burning,"[56] is not nearly as important as *how* these lines give voice to the present milieu. Eliot perceives the "quiet desperation"[57] that underlies a secular and technologically driven culture. His Tiresias, "though blind, throbbing between two lives,"[58] is *sacro* and *saecularis*, a hybrid who embodies both forces. A poem like *The*

---

[54] *The Waste Land* ln. 111

[55] *The Waste Land* ln. 115-116

[56] *The Waste Land* ln. 307-311

[57] From *Walden* (1854) - Henry David Thoreau

[58] *The Waste Land* ln. 218

Waste Land holds these tensions in play with remarkable precision. It perceives the narrative of progress and innovation, desolation and regress that defined the Twentieth Century. As Paul Simon would sing decades later, "These are the days of miracle and wonder, and don't cry baby, don't cry, don't cry."[59]

(2) I had not thought death had undone so many

Critics often describe Eliot's poetry as impersonal. The "Real Eliot" they argue is hidden behind a curtain of persona, concealed from the public like a wizard of Oz. In an age where social networking and a pornography of self-disclosure is the norm, Eliot is perceived as unusually reticent, with mannerisms thoroughly *better than thou.* Never mind that Eliot's entire notion of an objective correlative[60] considers how emotion is evoked through poetry, or that his poems endlessly seek moments of pathos and revelation: "Picnic / Lightning."[61] One can readily find an equally plausible reading of Eliot's demeanor and objective in his poetry. Consider sections two and four from *Preludes* (1917):

II

The morning comes to consciousness
Of faint stale smells of beer
From the sawdust-trampled street
With all its muddy feet that press
To early coffee-stands.

---

[59] "The Boy in the Bubble"- *Graceland* (1986)

[60] See "Hamlet and His Problems" (1919)

[61] *Lolita* - Vladimir Nabokov (1955)

With the other masquerades
That time resumes,
One thinks of all the hands
That are raising dingy shades
In a thousand furnished rooms.

IV

His soul stretched tight across the skies
That fade behind a city block,
Or trampled by insistent feet
At four and five and six o'clock;
And short square fingers stuffing pipes,
And evening newspapers, and eyes
Assured of certain certainties,
The conscience of a blackened street
Impatient to assume the world.

I am moved by fancies that are curled
Around these images, and cling:
The notion of some infinitely gentle
Infinitely suffering thing.

Wipe your hand across your mouth, and laugh;
The worlds revolve like ancient women
Gathering fuel in vacant lots.[62]

---

[62] *Preludes* ln. 14-23 / 39-54

Writing like this does not emerge from a disengaged talent. Eliot unflinchingly contemplates " . . . all the hands / That are raising dingy shades / In a thousand furnished rooms," with its suggestion of despondent communal and material decay. His vision of the "soul stretched tight against the skies" is a painful depiction of spiritual frailty and human suffering, as is his recognition elsewhere that " . . . human kind / Cannot bear very much reality."[63] To find deep feeling in Eliot, to apprehend his humanity, is to recognize his capacity to perceive the "deep heart's core"[64] in others, his ability to find kinship not just with the inhabitants of his time and place, but with the souls of history: Heraclitus is revered,[65] Phlebas is mourned,[66] and the walking dead of London are given a eulogy.[67] This is admirable in an age of callous dehumanization, and a tribute to Eliot's humility as an artist. He manages to employ a preternatural talent without drawing attention to his ego. It is never about him. The poem is the thing.

* * *

T.S. Eliot is a mandrake. The time to unearth his peculiar genius from the sediment is long overdue. Poems in this collection are drawn from his early career, with *The Waste Land*, *The Love Song of J. Alfred Prufrock*, *Gerontion*, and *Preludes* being the most notable. Readers are also encouraged to survey his later works to grasp the sum total of Eliot's ambitions. Four of Eliot's essays, including the seminal "Tradition and the Individual Talent" (1919) and "Hamlet and His Problems" (1919), accompany this volume as well. To read Eliot is to embrace his demands, to submit to his

---

[63] *Four Quartets - Burnt Norton* ln. 42-43

[64] See *The Lake Isle of Innisfree* - W.B. Yeats

[65] *Four Quartets - Epigraph*

[66] *The Waste Land - The Fire Sermon*

[67] *The Waste Land* ln. 60-68 / ln. 173-182

tutelage, and to marvel at the abiding power of the work itself, which sings as convincingly in this century as its own. Few authors can match Eliot's prophetic vision, his ear for the musicality of language, or what Craig Raine has called his "modernist interest in incompatible emotions."[68] Readers return to Eliot because his art attends to perennial human questions, and is singular in its appraisal of the human condition. The poetry, with its congruence and contradiction, assurance and anxiety, finds definition in a line from the Gospel of Mark: "I believe; help thou mine unbelief."

Jeremiah Webster
September 2013

[68] Raine pg. 63

THE WASTE LAND

"Nam Sibyllam quidem Cumis ego ipse oculis meis
vidi in ampulla pendere, et cum illi pueri dicerent:
Sibylla ti theleis; respondebat illa: apothanein thelo."

I. THE BURIAL OF THE DEAD

April is the cruellest month, breeding
Lilacs out of the dead land, mixing
Memory and desire, stirring
Dull roots with spring rain.
Winter kept us warm, covering
Earth in forgetful snow, feeding
A little life with dried tubers.
Summer surprised us, coming over the Starnbergersee
With a shower of rain; we stopped in the colonnade,
And went on in sunlight, into the Hofgarten,
And drank coffee, and talked for an hour.
Bin gar keine Russin, stamm' aus Litauen, echt deutsch.
And when we were children, staying at the archduke's,
My cousin's, he took me out on a sled,
And I was frightened. He said, Marie,
Marie, hold on tight. And down we went.
In the mountains, there you feel free.
I read, much of the night, and go south in the winter.

What are the roots that clutch, what branches grow
Out of this stony rubbish? Son of man,
You cannot say, or guess, for you know only
A heap of broken images, where the sun beats,
And the dead tree gives no shelter, the cricket no relief,
And the dry stone no sound of water. Only
There is shadow under this red rock,
(Come in under the shadow of this red rock),
And I will show you something different from either
Your shadow at morning striding behind you

Or your shadow at evening rising to meet you;
I will show you fear in a handful of dust.
Frisch weht der Wind
Der Heimat zu
Mein Irisch Kind,
Wo weilest du?
"You gave me hyacinths first a year ago;
"They called me the hyacinth girl."
—Yet when we came back, late, from the Hyacinth garden,
Your arms full, and your hair wet, I could not
Speak, and my eyes failed, I was neither
Living nor dead, and I knew nothing,
Looking into the heart of light, the silence.
Od' und leer das Meer.

Madame Sosostris, famous clairvoyante,
Had a bad cold, nevertheless
Is known to be the wisest woman in Europe,
With a wicked pack of cards. Here, said she,
Is your card, the drowned Phoenician Sailor,

(Those are pearls that were his eyes. Look!)
Here is Belladonna, the Lady of the Rocks,
The lady of situations.
Here is the man with three staves, and here the Wheel,
And here is the one-eyed merchant, and this card,
Which is blank, is something he carries on his back,
Which I am forbidden to see. I do not find
The Hanged Man. Fear death by water.
I see crowds of people, walking round in a ring.
Thank you. If you see dear Mrs. Equitone,
Tell her I bring the horoscope myself:
One must be so careful these days.

Unreal City,
Under the brown fog of a winter dawn,
A crowd flowed over London Bridge, so many,
I had not thought death had undone so many.
Sighs, short and infrequent, were exhaled,
And each man fixed his eyes before his feet.
Flowed up the hill and down King William Street,
To where Saint Mary Woolnoth kept the hours
With a dead sound on the final stroke of nine.
There I saw one I knew, and stopped him, crying "Stetson!
"You who were with me in the ships at Mylae!
"That corpse you planted last year in your garden,
"Has it begun to sprout? Will it bloom this year?
"Or has the sudden frost disturbed its bed?

"Oh keep the Dog far hence, that's friend to men,
"Or with his nails he'll dig it up again!
"You! *hypocrite lecteur!— mon semblable,— mon frere!*"

II. A GAME OF CHESS

The Chair she sat in, like a burnished throne,
Glowed on the marble, where the glass
Held up by standards wrought with fruited vines
From which a golden Cupidon peeped out
(Another hid his eyes behind his wing)
Doubled the flames of sevenbranched candelabra
Reflecting light upon the table as
The glitter of her jewels rose to meet it,
From satin cases poured in rich profusion;
In vials of ivory and coloured glass
Unstoppered, lurked her strange synthetic perfumes,
Unguent, powdered, or liquid— troubled, confused
And drowned the sense in odours; stirred by the air
That freshened from the window, these ascended
In fattening the prolonged candle-flames,
Flung their smoke into the laquearia,
Stirring the pattern on the coffered ceiling.
Huge sea-wood fed with copper
Burned green and orange, framed by the coloured stone,
In which sad light a carved dolphin swam.
Above the antique mantel was displayed
As though a window gave upon the sylvan scene
The change of Philomel, by the barbarous king
So rudely forced; yet there the nightingale
Filled all the desert with inviolable voice
And still she cried, and still the world pursues,

"Jug Jug" to dirty ears.
And other withered stumps of time
Were told upon the walls; staring forms
Leaned out, leaning, hushing the room enclosed.
Footsteps shuffled on the stair.
Under the firelight, under the brush, her hair
Spread out in fiery points
Glowed into words, then would be savagely still.

"My nerves are bad to-night. Yes, bad. Stay with me.
"Speak to me. Why do you never speak. Speak.
"What are you thinking of? What thinking? What?
"I never know what you are thinking. Think."

I think we are in rats' alley
Where the dead men lost their bones.

"What is that noise?"
                    The wind under the door.
"What is that noise now? What is the wind doing?"
                    Nothing again nothing.
                                        "Do
You know nothing? Do you see nothing? Do you remember
Nothing?"
        I remember
            Those are pearls that were his eyes.
"Are you alive, or not? Is there nothing in your head?"
                                But
O O O O that Shakespeherian Rag—
It's so elegant
So intelligent

"What shall I do now? What shall I do?"
I shall rush out as I am, and walk the street
"With my hair down, so. What shall we do to-morrow?
"What shall we ever do?"
                                        The hot water at ten.
And if it rains, a closed car at four.
And we shall play a game of chess,
Pressing lidless eyes and waiting for a knock upon the door.

When Lil's husband got demobbed, I said—
I didn't mince my words, I said to her myself,
HURRY UP PLEASE ITS TIME
Now Albert's coming back, make yourself a bit smart.
He'll want to know what you done with that money he gave you
To get yourself some teeth. He did, I was there.
You have them all out, Lil, and get a nice set,
He said, I swear, I can't bear to look at you.
And no more can't I, I said, and think of poor Albert,
He's been in the army four years, he wants a good time,
And if you don't give it him, there's others will, I said.
Oh is there, she said. Something o' that, I said.
Then I'll know who to thank, she said, and give me a straight look.
HURRY UP PLEASE ITS TIME
If you don't like it you can get on with it, I said.
Others can pick and choose if you can't.
But if Albert makes off, it won't be for lack of telling.
You ought to be ashamed, I said, to look so antique.
(And her only thirty-one.)
I can't help it, she said, pulling a long face,
It's them pills I took, to bring it off, she said.

(She's had five already, and nearly died of young George.)
The chemist said it would be alright, but I've never been the same.
You *are* a proper fool, I said.
Well, if Albert won't leave you alone, there it is, I said,
What you get married for if you don't want children?
HURRY UP PLEASE ITS TIME
Well, that Sunday Albert was home, they had a hot gammon,
And they asked me in to dinner, to get the beauty of it hot—
HURRY UP PLEASE ITS TIME
HURRY UP PLEASE ITS TIME
Goonight Bill. Goonight Lou. Goonight May. Goonight.
Ta ta. Goonight. Goonight.
Good night, ladies, good night, sweet ladies, good night, good night.

III. THE FIRE SERMON

The river's tent is broken: the last fingers of leaf
Clutch and sink into the wet bank. The wind
Crosses the brown land, unheard. The nymphs are departed.
Sweet Thames, run softly, till I end my song.
The river bears no empty bottles, sandwich papers,
Silk handkerchiefs, cardboard boxes, cigarette ends
Or other testimony of summer nights. The nymphs are departed.
And their friends, the loitering heirs of city directors;
Departed, have left no addresses.
By the waters of Leman I sat down and wept . . .
Sweet Thames, run softly till I end my song,
Sweet Thames, run softly, for I speak not loud or long.
But at my back in a cold blast I hear
The rattle of the bones, and chuckle spread from ear to ear.

A rat crept softly through the vegetation
Dragging its slimy belly on the bank
While I was fishing in the dull canal
On a winter evening round behind the gashouse
Musing upon the king my brother's wreck
And on the king my father's death before him.
White bodies naked on the low damp ground
And bones cast in a little low dry garret,
Rattled by the rat's foot only, year to year.
But at my back from time to time I hear
The sound of horns and motors, which shall bring

Sweeney to Mrs. Porter in the spring.
O the moon shone bright on Mrs. Porter
And on her daughter
They wash their feet in soda water
Et O ces voix d'enfants, chantant dans la coupole!

Twit twit twit
Jug jug jug jug jug jug
So rudely forc'd.
Tereu
Unreal City
Under the brown fog of a winter noon
Mr. Eugenides, the Smyrna merchant
Unshaven, with a pocket full of currants
C.i.f. London: documents at sight,
Asked me in demotic French
To luncheon at the Cannon Street Hotel
Followed by a weekend at the Metropole.

At the violet hour, when the eyes and back
Turn upward from the desk, when the human engine waits
Like a taxi throbbing waiting,
I Tiresias, though blind, throbbing between two lives,
Old man with wrinkled female breasts, can see
At the violet hour, the evening hour that strives
Homeward, and brings the sailor home from sea,
The typist home at teatime, clears her breakfast, lights
Her stove, and lays out food in tins.
Out of the window perilously spread
Her drying combinations touched by the sun's last rays,
On the divan are piled (at night her bed)

Stockings, slippers, camisoles, and stays.
I Tiresias, old man with wrinkled dugs
Perceived the scene, and foretold the rest—
I too awaited the expected guest.
He, the young man carbuncular, arrives,
A small house agent's clerk, with one bold stare,
One of the low on whom assurance sits
As a silk hat on a Bradford millionaire.
The time is now propitious, as he guesses,
The meal is ended, she is bored and tired,
Endeavours to engage her in caresses
Which still are unreproved, if undesired.
Flushed and decided, he assaults at once;
Exploring hands encounter no defence;
His vanity requires no response,
And makes a welcome of indifference.
(And I Tiresias have foresuffered all
Enacted on this same divan or bed;
I who have sat by Thebes below the wall
And walked among the lowest of the dead.)
Bestows one final patronising kiss,
And gropes his way, finding the stairs unlit . . .

She turns and looks a moment in the glass,
Hardly aware of her departed lover;
Her brain allows one half-formed thought to pass:
"Well now that's done: and I'm glad it's over."
When lovely woman stoops to folly and
Paces about her room again, alone,
She smoothes her hair with automatic hand,
And puts a record on the gramophone.

"This music crept by me upon the waters"
And along the Strand, up Queen Victoria Street.
O City city, I can sometimes hear
Beside a public bar in Lower Thames Street,
The pleasant whining of a mandoline
And a clatter and a chatter from within
Where fishmen lounge at noon: where the walls
Of Magnus Martyr hold
Inexplicable splendour of Ionian white and gold.

The river sweats
Oil and tar
The barges drift
With the turning tide
Red sails
Wide
To leeward, swing on the heavy spar.
The barges wash
Drifting logs
Down Greenwich reach
Past the Isle of Dogs.
        Weialala leia
        Wallala leialala

Elizabeth and Leicester
Beating oars
The stern was formed
A gilded shell
Red and gold
The brisk swell

Rippled both shores
Southwest wind
Carried down stream
The peal of bells
White towers
        Weialala leia
        Wallala leialala

"Trams and dusty trees.
Highbury bore me. Richmond and Kew
Undid me. By Richmond I raised my knees
Supine on the floor of a narrow canoe."

"My feet are at Moorgate, and my heart
Under my feet. After the event
He wept. He promised 'a new start'.
I made no comment. What should I resent?"
"On Margate Sands.
I can connect
Nothing with nothing.
The broken fingernails of dirty hands.
My people humble people who expect
Nothing."
    la la
To Carthage then I came

Burning burning burning burning
O Lord Thou pluckest me out
O Lord Thou pluckest

burning

IV. DEATH BY WATER

Phlebas the Phoenician, a fortnight dead,
Forgot the cry of gulls, and the deep sea swell
And the profit and loss.
                    A current under sea
Picked his bones in whispers. As he rose and fell
He passed the stages of his age and youth
Entering the whirlpool.
                    Gentile or Jew
O you who turn the wheel and look to windward,
Consider Phlebas, who was once handsome and tall as you.

V. WHAT THE THUNDER SAID

After the torchlight red on sweaty faces
After the frosty silence in the gardens
After the agony in stony places
The shouting and the crying
Prison and palace and reverberation
Of thunder of spring over distant mountains
He who was living is now dead
We who were living are now dying
With a little patience

Here is no water but only rock
Rock and no water and the sandy road
The road winding above among the mountains
Which are mountains of rock without water
If there were water we should stop and drink
Amongst the rock one cannot stop or think
Sweat is dry and feet are in the sand
If there were only water amongst the rock
Dead mountain mouth of carious teeth that cannot spit
Here one can neither stand nor lie nor sit
There is not even silence in the mountains
But dry sterile thunder without rain
There is not even solitude in the mountains
But red sullen faces sneer and snarl
From doors of mud-cracked houses
                                        If there were water

And no rock
If there were rock
And also water
And water
A spring
A pool among the rock
If there were the sound of water only
Not the cicada
And dry grass singing
But sound of water over a rock
Where the hermit-thrush sings in the pine trees
Drip drop drip drop drop drop drop
But there is no water

Who is the third who walks always beside you?
When I count, there are only you and I together
But when I look ahead up the white road
There is always another one walking beside you
Gliding wrapt in a brown mantle, hooded
I do not know whether a man or a woman
—But who is that on the other side of you?

What is that sound high in the air
Murmur of maternal lamentation
Who are those hooded hordes swarming
Over endless plains, stumbling in cracked earth
Ringed by the flat horizon only
What is the city over the mountains
Cracks and reforms and bursts in the violet air
Falling towers
Jerusalem Athens Alexandria
Vienna London

Unreal

A woman drew her long black hair out tight
And fiddled whisper music on those strings
And bats with baby faces in the violet light
Whistled, and beat their wings
And crawled head downward down a blackened wall
And upside down in air were towers
Tolling reminiscent bells, that kept the hours
And voices singing out of empty cisterns and exhausted wells.

In this decayed hole among the mountains
In the faint moonlight, the grass is singing
Over the tumbled graves, about the chapel
There is the empty chapel, only the wind's home.
It has no windows, and the door swings,
Dry bones can harm no one.
Only a cock stood on the rooftree
Co co rico co co rico
In a flash of lightning. Then a damp gust
Bringing rain

Ganga was sunken, and the limp leaves
Waited for rain, while the black clouds
Gathered far distant, over Himavant.
The jungle crouched, humped in silence.
Then spoke the thunder
DA
Datta: what have we given?
My friend, blood shaking my heart
The awful daring of a moment's surrender
Which an age of prudence can never retract

By this, and this only, we have existed
Which is not to be found in our obituaries
Or in memories draped by the beneficent spider
Or under seals broken by the lean solicitor
In our empty rooms
DA
Dayadhvam: I have heard the key
Turn in the door once and turn once only
We think of the key, each in his prison
Thinking of the key, each confirms a prison
Only at nightfall, aetherial rumours
Revive for a moment a broken Coriolanus
DA
Damyata: The boat responded
Gaily, to the hand expert with sail and oar
The sea was calm, your heart would have responded
Gaily, when invited, beating obedient
To controlling hands

                    I sat upon the shore
Fishing, with the arid plain behind me
Shall I at least set my lands in order?

London Bridge is falling down falling down falling down

Poi s'ascose nel foco che gli affina
Quando fiam ceu chelidon— O swallow swallow
Le Prince d'Aquitaine a la tour abolie
These fragments I have shored against my ruins
Why then Ile fit you. Hieronymo's mad againe.
Datta. Dayadhvam. Damyata.
        Shantih   shantih   shantih

NOTES ON "THE WASTE LAND"

Not only the title, but the plan and a good deal of the incidental symbolism of the poem were suggested by Miss Jessie L. Weston's book on the Grail legend: *From Ritual to Romance* (Macmillan). Indeed, so deeply am I indebted, Miss Weston's book will elucidate the difficulties of the poem much better than my notes can do; and I recommend it (apart from the great interest of the book itself) to any who think such elucidation of the poem worth the trouble. To another work of anthropology I am indebted in general, one which has influenced our generation profoundly; I mean *The Golden Bough*; I have used especially the two volumes *Adonis, Attis, Osiris.* Anyone who is acquainted with these works will immediately recognise in the poem certain references to vegetation ceremonies.

I. THE BURIAL OF THE DEAD

Line 20. Cf. Ezekiel 2:1.

23. Cf. Ecclesiastes 12:5.

31. V. *Tristan und Isolde*, i, verses 5-8.

42. Id. iii, verse 24.

46. I am not familiar with the exact constitution of the Tarot pack of cards, from which I have obviously departed to suit my own convenience. The Hanged Man, a member of the traditional pack, fits my purpose in two ways: because he is associated in my mind with the Hanged God of Frazer, and because I associate him with the hooded figure in the passage of the disciples to Emmaus in Part V. The Phoenician Sailor and the Merchant appear later; also the "crowds of people," and Death by Water is executed in Part IV. The Man with Three Staves (an authentic member of the Tarot pack) I associate, quite arbitrarily, with the Fisher King himself.

60. Cf. Baudelaire:

"Fourmillante cite;, cite; pleine de reves,
Ou le spectre en plein jour raccroche le passant."

63. Cf. *Inferno*, iii. 55-7.

"si lunga tratta
di gente, ch'io non avrei mai creduto
che morte tanta n'avesse disfatta."

64. Cf. *Inferno*, iv. 25-7:
"Quivi, secondo che per ascoltare,
"non avea pianto, ma' che di sospiri,
"che l'aura eterna facevan tremare."

68. A phenomenon which I have often noticed.

74. Cf. the Dirge in Webster's *White Devil* .

76. V. Baudelaire, Preface to *Fleurs du Mal.*

II. A GAME OF CHESS

77. Cf. *Antony and Cleopatra*, II. ii., l. 190.

92. Laquearia. V. *Aeneid*, I. 726:
dependent lychni laquearibus aureis incensi, et noctem flammis funalia vincunt.

98. Sylvan scene. V. Milton, *Paradise Lost*, iv. 140.

99. V. Ovid, *Metamorphoses*, vi, Philomela.

100. Cf. Part III, l. 204.

115. Cf. Part III, l. 195.

118. Cf. Webster: "Is the wind in that door still?"

126. Cf. Part I, l. 37, 48.

138. Cf. the game of chess in Middleton's *Women beware Women.*

III. THE FIRE SERMON

176. V. Spenser, *Prothalamion.*

192. Cf. *The Tempest*, I. ii.

196. Cf. Marvell, *To His Coy Mistress.*

197. Cf. Day, *Parliament of Bees*:

"When of the sudden, listening, you shall hear,
"A noise of horns and hunting, which shall bring
"Actaeon to Diana in the spring,
"Where all shall see her naked skin . . ."

199. I do not know the origin of the ballad from which these lines are taken: it was reported to me from Sydney, Australia.

202. V. Verlaine, *Parsifal.*

210. The currants were quoted at a price "carriage and insurance free to London"; and the Bill of Lading etc. were to be handed to the buyer upon payment of the sight draft.

210. "Carriage and insurance free"] "cost, insurance and freight"-Editor.

218. Tiresias, although a mere spectator and not indeed a "character," is yet the most important personage in the poem, uniting all the rest. Just as the one-eyed merchant, seller of currants, melts into the Phoenician Sailor, and the latter is not wholly distinct from Ferdinand Prince of Naples, so all the women are one woman, and the two sexes meet in Tiresias. What Tiresias sees, in fact, is the substance of the poem. The whole passage from Ovid is of great anthropological interest:

'. . . Cum Iunone iocos et maior vestra profecto est
Quam, quae contingit maribus,' dixisse, 'voluptas.'
Illa negat; placuit quae sit sententia docti
Quaerere Tiresiae: venus huic erat utraque nota.
Nam duo magnorum viridi coeuntia silva
Corpora serpentum baculi violaverat ictu
Deque viro factus, mirabile, femina septem
Egerat autumnos; octavo rursus eosdem
Vidit et 'est vestrae si tanta potentia plagae,'
Dixit 'ut auctoris sortem in contraria mutet,
Nunc quoque vos feriam!' percussis anguibus isdem
Forma prior rediit genetivaque venit imago.
Arbiter hic igitur sumptus de lite iocosa
Dicta Iovis firmat; gravius Saturnia iusto
Nec pro materia fertur doluisse suique

Iudicis aeterna damnavit lumina nocte,
At pater omnipotens (neque enim licet inrita cuiquam
Facta dei fecisse deo) pro lumine adempto
Scire futura dedit poenamque levavit honore.

221. This may not appear as exact as Sappho's lines, but I had in mind the "longshore" or "dory" fisherman, who returns at nightfall.

253. V. Goldsmith, the song in *The Vicar of Wakefield.*

257. V. *The Tempest*, as above.

264. The interior of St. Magnus Martyr is to my mind one of the finest among Wren's interiors. See *The Proposed Demolition of Nineteen City Churches* (P. S. King & Son, Ltd.).

266. The Song of the (three) Thames-daughters begins here. From line 292 to 306 inclusive they speak in turn.
V. *Gutterdsammerung*, III. i: the Rhine-daughters.
279. V. Froude, *Elizabeth*, Vol. I, ch. iv, letter of De Quadra to Philip of Spain:

"In the afternoon we were in a barge, watching the games on the river. (The queen) was alone with Lord Robert and myself on the poop, when they began to talk nonsense, and went so far that Lord Robert at last said, as I was on the spot there was no reason why they should not be married if the queen pleased."

293. Cf. *Purgatorio*, v. 133:

"Ricorditi di me, che son la Pia;
Siena mi fe', disfecemi Maremma."

307. V. St. Augustine's *Confessions*: "to Carthage then I came, where a cauldron of unholy loves sang all about mine ears."

308. The complete text of the Buddha's Fire Sermon (which corresponds in importance to the Sermon on the Mount) from which these words are taken, will be found translated in the late Henry Clarke Warren's *Buddhism in Translation* (Harvard Oriental Series). Mr. Warren was one of the great pioneers of Buddhist studies in the Occident.

309. From St. Augustine's *Confessions* again. The collocation of these two representatives of eastern and western asceticism, as the culmination of this part of the poem, is not an accident.

V. WHAT THE THUNDER SAID

In the first part of Part V three themes are employed: the journey to Emmaus, the approach to the Chapel Perilous (see Miss Weston's book) and the present decay of eastern Europe.

357. This is *Turdus aonalaschkae pallasii*, the hermit-thrush which I have heard in Quebec County. Chapman says (*Handbook of Birds of Eastern North America*) "it is most at home in secluded woodland and thickety retreats. . . . Its notes are not remarkable for variety or volume, but in purity and sweetness of tone and exquisite modulation they are unequalled." Its "water-dripping song" is justly celebrated.

360. The following lines were stimulated by the account of one of the Antarctic expeditions (I forget which, but I think one of Shackleton's): it was related that the party of explorers, at the extremity of their strength, had the constant delusion that there was *one more member* than could actually be counted.

367-77. Cf. Hermann Hesse, *Blick ins Chaos*:
"Schon ist halb Europa, schon ist zumindest der halbe Osten Europas auf dem Wege zum Chaos, fährt betrunken im heiligem Wahn am Abgrund entlang und singt dazu, singt betrunken und hymnisch wie Dmitri Karamasoff sang. Ueber diese Lieder lacht der Bürger beleidigt, der Heilige und Seher hört sie mit Tränen."

402. "Datta, dayadhvam, damyata" (Give, sympathize, control). The fable of the meaning of the Thunder is found in the Brihadaranyaka-Upanishad, 5, 1. A translation is found in Deussen's Sechzig Upanishads des Veda, p. 489.

408. Cf. Webster, *The White Devil*, v. vi:

"... they'll remarry
Ere the worm pierce your winding-sheet, ere the spider
Make a thin curtain for your epitaphs."

412. Cf. *Inferno*, xxxiii. 46:

"ed io sentii chiavar l'uscio di sotto
all'orribile torre."

Also F. H. Bradley, *Appearance and Reality*, p. 346:

"My external sensations are no less private to myself than are my thoughts or my feelings. In either case my experience falls within my own circle, a circle closed on the outside; and, with all its elements alike, every sphere is opaque to the others which surround it. . . . In brief, regarded as an existence which appears in a soul, the whole world for each is peculiar and private to that soul."

425. V. Weston, *From Ritual to Romance*; chapter on the Fisher King.

428. V. *Purgatorio*, xxvi. 148.

> "'Ara vos prec per aquella valor
> 'que vos guida al som de l'escalina,
> 'sovegna vos a temps de ma dolor.'
> Poi s'ascose nel foco che gli affina."

429. V. *Pervigilium Veneris*. Cf. Philomela in Parts II and III.

430. V. Gerard de Nerval, Sonnet *El Desdichado*.

432. V. Kyd's *Spanish Tragedy*.

434. Shantih. Repeated as here, a formal ending to an Upanishad. 'The Peace which passeth understanding' is a feeble translation of the content of this word.

Gerontion

Thou hast nor youth nor age
But as it were an after dinner sleep
Dreaming of both.

Here I am, an old man in a dry month,
Being read to by a boy, waiting for rain.
I was neither at the hot gates
Nor fought in the warm rain
Nor knee deep in the salt marsh, heaving a cutlass,
Bitten by flies, fought.
My house is a decayed house,
And the jew squats on the window sill, the owner,
Spawned in some estaminet of Antwerp,
Blistered in Brussels, patched and peeled in London.
The goat coughs at night in the field overhead;
Rocks, moss, stonecrop, iron, merds.
The woman keeps the kitchen, makes tea,
Sneezes at evening, poking the peevish gutter.
I an old man,
A dull head among windy spaces.

Signs are taken for wonders. "We would see a sign!":
The word within a word, unable to speak a word,
Swaddled with darkness. In the juvescence of the year
Came Christ the tiger

In depraved May, dogwood and chestnut, flowering judas,
To be eaten, to be divided, to be drunk
Among whispers; by Mr. Silvero
With caressing hands, at Limoges
Who walked all night in the next room;
By Hakagawa, bowing among the Titians;
By Madame de Tornquist, in the dark room
Shifting the candles; Fraulein von Kulp
Who turned in the hall, one hand on the door. Vacant shuttles
Weave the wind. I have no ghosts,
An old man in a draughty house
Under a windy knob.

After such knowledge, what forgiveness? Think now
History has many cunning passages, contrived corridors
And issues, deceives with whispering ambitions,
Guides us by vanities. Think now
She gives when our attention is distracted
And what she gives, gives with such supple confusions
That the giving famishes the craving. Gives too late
What's not believed in, or if still believed,
In memory only, reconsidered passion. Gives too soon
Into weak hands, what's thought can be dispensed with
Till the refusal propagates a fear. Think
Neither fear nor courage saves us. Unnatural vices
Are fathered by our heroism. Virtues
Are forced upon us by our impudent crimes.
These tears are shaken from the wrath-bearing tree.

The tiger springs in the new year. Us he devours. Think at last
We have not reached conclusion, when I

Stiffen in a rented house. Think at last
I have not made this show purposelessly
And it is not by any concitation
Of the backward devils.

I would meet you upon this honestly.
I that was near your heart was removed therefrom
To lose beauty in terror, terror in inquisition.
I have lost my passion: why should I need to keep it
Since what is kept must be adulterated?
I have lost my sight, smell, hearing, taste and touch:
How should I use it for your closer contact?

These with a thousand small deliberations
Protract the profit of their chilled delirium,
Excite the membrane, when the sense has cooled,
With pungent sauces, multiply variety
In a wilderness of mirrors. What will the spider do,
Suspend its operations, will the weevil
Delay? De Bailhache, Fresca, Mrs. Cammel, whirled
Beyond the circuit of the shuddering Bear
In fractured atoms. Gull against the wind, in the windy straits
Of Belle Isle, or running on the Horn,
White feathers in the snow, the Gulf claims,
And an old man driven by the Trades
To a sleepy corner.

Tenants of the house,
Thoughts of a dry brain in a dry season.

Burbank with a Baedeker: Bleistein with a Cigar

Tra-la-la-la-la-laire—nil nisi divinum stabile est; caetera fumus—the gondola stopped, the old palace was there, how charming its grey and pink—goats and monkeys, with such hair too!—so the countess passed on until she came through the little park, where Niobe presented her with a cabinet, and so departed.

Burbank crossed a little bridge
Descending at a small hotel;
Princess Volupine arrived,
They were together, and he fell.

Defunctive music under sea
Passed seaward with the passing bell
Slowly: the God Hercules
Had left him, that had loved him well.

The horses, under the axletree
Beat up the dawn from Istria
With even feet. Her shuttered barge
Burned on the water all the day.

But this or such was Bleistein's way:
A saggy bending of the knees
And elbows, with the palms turned out,
Chicago Semite Viennese.

A lustreless protrusive eye
Stares from the protozoic slime
At a perspective of Canaletto.
The smoky candle end of time

Declines. On the Rialto once.
The rats are underneath the piles.
The jew is underneath the lot.
Money in furs. The boatman smiles,

Princess Volupine extends
A meagre, blue-nailed, phthisic hand
To climb the waterstair. Lights, lights,
She entertains Sir Ferdinand

Klein. Who clipped the lion's wings
And flea'd his rump and pared his claws?
Thought Burbank, meditating on
Time's ruins, and the seven laws.

Sweeney Erect

And the trees about me,
Let them be dry and leafless; let the rocks
Groan with continual surges; and behind me
Make all a desolation. Look, look, wenches!
Paint me a cavernous waste shore
Cast in the unstilted Cyclades,
Paint me the bold anfractuous rocks
Faced by the snarled and yelping seas.

Display me Aeolus above
Reviewing the insurgent gales
Which tangle Ariadne's hair
And swell with haste the perjured sails.

Morning stirs the feet and hands
(Nausicaa and Polypheme),
Gesture of orang-outang
Rises from the sheets in steam.

This withered root of knots of hair
Slitted below and gashed with eyes,
This oval O cropped out with teeth:
The sickle motion from the thighs

Jackknifes upward at the knees
Then straightens out from heel to hip

Pushing the framework of the bed
And clawing at the pillow slip.

Sweeney addressed full length to shave
Broadbottomed, pink from nape to base,
Knows the female temperament
And wipes the suds around his face.

(The lengthened shadow of a man
Is history, said Emerson
Who had not seen the silhouette
Of Sweeney straddled in the sun).

Tests the razor on his leg
Waiting until the shriek subsides.
The epileptic on the bed
Curves backward, clutching at her sides.

The ladies of the corridor
Find themselves involved, disgraced,
Call witness to their principles
And deprecate the lack of taste

Observing that hysteria
Might easily be misunderstood;
Mrs. Turner intimates
It does the house no sort of good.

But Doris, towelled from the bath,
Enters padding on broad feet,
Bringing sal volatile
And a glass of brandy neat.

A Cooking Egg

En l'an trentiesme de mon aage
Que toutes mes hontes j'ay beues...
Pipit sate upright in her chair
Some distance from where I was sitting;
Views of the Oxford Colleges
Lay on the table, with the knitting.

Daguerreotypes and silhouettes,
Her grandfather and great great aunts,
Supported on the mantelpiece
An Invitation to the Dance.

. . . . . .

I shall not want Honour in Heaven
For I shall meet Sir Philip Sidney
And have talk with Coriolanus
And other heroes of that kidney.

I shall not want Capital in Heaven
For I shall meet Sir Alfred Mond:
We two shall lie together, lapt
In a five per cent Exchequer Bond.

I shall not want Society in Heaven,
Lucretia Borgia shall be my Bride;
Her anecdotes will be more amusing
Than Pipit's experience could provide.

I shall not want Pipit in Heaven:
  Madame Blavatsky will instruct me
In the Seven Sacred Trances;
  Piccarda de Donati will conduct me.

. . . . . .

But where is the penny world I bought
  To eat with Pipit behind the screen?
The red-eyed scavengers are creeping
  From Kentish Town and Golder's Green;

Where are the eagles and the trumpets?

  Buried beneath some snow-deep Alps.
Over buttered scones and crumpets
  Weeping, weeping multitudes
Droop in a hundred A.B.C.'s

["ABC's" signifes endemic teashops, found in all parts of London. The initials signify "Aerated Bread Company, Limited."]

The Hippopotamus

> Similiter et omnes revereantur Diaconos, ut mandatum Jesu Christi; et Episcopum, ut Jesum Christum, existentem filium Patris; Presbyteros autem, ut concilium Dei et conjunctionem Apostolorum. Sine his Ecclesia non vocatur; de quibus suadeo vos sic habeo.

S. IGNATII AD TRALLIANOS.

And when this epistle is read among you, cause that it be read also in the church of the Laodiceans.

The broad-backed hippopotamus
Rests on his belly in the mud;
Although he seems so firm to us
He is merely flesh and blood.

Flesh-and-blood is weak and frail,
Susceptible to nervous shock;
While the True Church can never fail
For it is based upon a rock.

The hippo's feeble steps may err
In compassing material ends,
While the True Church need never stir
To gather in its dividends.

The 'potamus can never reach
The mango on the mango-tree;
But fruits of pomegranate and peach
Refresh the Church from over sea.

At mating time the hippo's voice
Betrays inflexions hoarse and odd,
But every week we hear rejoice
The Church, at being one with God.

The hippopotamus's day
Is passed in sleep; at night he hunts;
God works in a mysterious way-
The Church can sleep and feed at once.

I saw the 'potamus take wing
Ascending from the damp savannas,
And quiring angels round him sing
The praise of God, in loud hosannas.

Blood of the Lamb shall wash him clean
And him shall heavenly arms enfold,
Among the saints he shall be seen
Performing on a harp of gold.

He shall be washed as white as snow,
By all the martyr'd virgins kiss,
While the True Church remains below
Wrapt in the old miasmal mist.

Dans le Restaurant

Le garcon délabré qui n'a rien à faire
Que de se gratter les doigts et se pencher sur mon épaule:
"Dans mon pays il fera temps pluvieux,
Du vent, du grand soleil, et de la pluie;
C'est ce qu'on appelle le jour de lessive des gueux."
(Bavard, baveux, à la croupe arrondie,
Je te prie, au moins, ne bave pas dans la soupe).
"Les saules trempés, et des bourgeons sur les ronces—
C'est là, dans une averse, qu'on s'abrite.
J'avais septtans, elle était plus petite.
Elle etait toute mouillée, je lui ai donné des primavères."
Les tâches de son gilet montent au chiffre de trente-huit.
"Je la chatouillais, pour la faire rire.
J'éprouvais un instant de puissance et de délire."

Mais alors, vieux lubrique, a cet âge...
"Monsieur, le fait est dur.
Il est venu, nous peloter, un gros chien;
Moi j'avais peur, je l'ai quittee a mi-chemin.
C'est dommage."

Mais alors, tu as ton vautour!
Va t'en te décrotter les rides du visage;
Tiens, ma fourchette, décrasse-toi le crâne.
De quel droit payes-tu des expériences comme moi?
Tiens, voilà dix sous, pour la salle-de-bains.

Phlébas, le Phénicien, pendant quinze jours noyé,
Oubliait les cris des mouettes et la houle de Cornouaille,
Et les profits et les pertes, et la cargaison d'etain:
Un courant de sous-mer l'emporta tres loin,
Le repassant aux étapes de sa vie antérieure.
Figurez-vous donc, c'etait un sort penible;
Cependant, ce fut jadis un bel homme, de haute taille.

Whispers of Immortality

Webster was much possessed by death
And saw the skull beneath the skin;
And breastless creatures under ground
Leaned backward with a lipless grin.

Daffodil bulbs instead of balls
Stared from the sockets of the eyes!
He knew that thought clings round dead limbs
Tightening its lusts and luxuries.

Donne, I suppose, was such another
Who found no substitute for sense;
To seize and clutch and penetrate,
Expert beyond experience,

He knew the anguish of the marrow
The ague of the skeleton;
No contact possible to flesh
Allayed the fever of the bone.

. . . . .

Grishkin is nice: her Russian eye
Is underlined for emphasis;
Uncorseted, her friendly bust
Gives promise of pneumatic bliss.

The couched Brazilian jaguar
Compels the scampering marmoset
With subtle effluence of cat;
Grishkin has a maisonette;

The sleek Brazilian jaguar
Does not in its arboreal gloom
Distil so rank a feline smell
As Grishkin in a drawing-room.

And even the Abstract Entities
Circumambulate her charm;
But our lot crawls between dry ribs
To keep our metaphysics warm.

Sweeney Among the Nightingales

Apeneck Sweeney spreads his knees
Letting his arms hang down to laugh,
The zebra stripes along his jaw
Swelling to maculate giraffe.

The circles of the stormy moon
Slide westward toward the River Plate,
Death and the Raven drift above
And Sweeney guards the hornèd gate.

Gloomy Orion and the Dog
Are veiled; and hushed the shrunken seas;
The person in the Spanish cape
Tries to sit on Sweeney's knees

Slips and pulls the table cloth
Overturns a coffee-cup,
Reorganized upon the floor
She yawns and draws a stocking up;

The silent man in mocha brown
Sprawls at the window-sill and gapes;
The waiter brings in oranges
Bananas figs and hothouse grapes;

The silent vertebrate in brown
Contracts and concentrates, withdraws;
Rachel née Rabinovitch
Tears at the grapes with murderous paws;

She and the lady in the cape
Are suspect, thought to be in league;
Therefore the man with heavy eyes
Declines the gambit, shows fatigue,

Leaves the room and reappears
Outside the window, leaning in,
Branches of wisteria
Circumscribe a golden grin;

The host with someone indistinct
Converses at the door apart,
The nightingales are singing near
The Convent of the Sacred Heart,

And sang within the bloody wood
When Agamemnon cried aloud,
And let their liquid droppings fall
To stain the stiff dishonoured shroud.

The Love Song of J. Alfred Prufrock

S'io credesse che mia risposta fosse
A persona che mai tornasse al mondo,
Questa fiamma staria senza piu scosse.
Ma perciocche giammai di questo fondo
Non torno vivo alcun, s'i'odo il vero,
Senza tema d'infamia ti rispondo.

Let us go then, you and I,
When the evening is spread out against the sky
Like a patient etherized upon a table;
Let us go, through certain half-deserted streets,
The muttering retreats
Of restless nights in one-night cheap hotels
And sawdust restaurants with oyster-shells:
Streets that follow like a tedious argument
Of insidious intent
To lead you to an overwhelming question....
Oh, do not ask, "What is it?"
Let us go and make our visit.

In the room the women come and go
Talking of Michelangelo.

The yellow fog that rubs its back upon the window-panes,
The yellow smoke that rubs its muzzle on the window-panes
Licked its tongue into the corners of the evening,
Lingered upon the pools that stand in drains,
Let fall upon its back the soot that falls from chimneys,

Slipped by the terrace, made a sudden leap,
And seeing that it was a soft October night,
Curled once about the house, and fell asleep.

And indeed there will be time
For the yellow smoke that slides along the street,
Rubbing its back upon the window panes;
There will be time, there will be time
To prepare a face to meet the faces that you meet
There will be time to murder and create,
And time for all the works and days of hands
That lift and drop a question on your plate;
Time for you and time for me,
And time yet for a hundred indecisions,
And for a hundred visions and revisions,
Before the taking of a toast and tea.

In the room the women come and go
Talking of Michelangelo.

And indeed there will be time
To wonder, "Do I dare?" and, "Do I dare?"
Time to turn back and descend the stair,
With a bald spot in the middle of my hair—
(They will say: "How his hair is growing thin!")
My morning coat, my collar mounting firmly to the chin,
My necktie rich and modest, but asserted by a simple pin—
(They will say: "But how his arms and legs are thin!")
Do I dare
Disturb the universe?
In a minute there is time
For decisions and revisions which a minute will reverse.

For I have known them all already, known them all:
Have known the evenings, mornings, afternoons,
I have measured out my life with coffee spoons;
I know the voices dying with a dying fall
Beneath the music from a farther room.
  So how should I presume?

And I have known the eyes already, known them all—
The eyes that fix you in a formulated phrase,
And when I am formulated, sprawling on a pin,
When I am pinned and wriggling on the wall,
Then how should I begin
To spit out all the butt-ends of my days and ways?
  And how should I presume?

And I have known the arms already, known them all—
Arms that are braceleted and white and bare
(But in the lamplight, downed with light brown hair!)
Is it perfume from a dress
That makes me so digress?
Arms that lie along a table, or wrap about a shawl.
  And should I then presume?
  And how should I begin?

. . . .

Shall I say, I have gone at dusk through narrow streets
And watched the smoke that rises from the pipes
Of lonely men in shirt-sleeves, leaning out of windows?

I should have been a pair of ragged claws
Scuttling across the floors of silent seas.

. . . .

And the afternoon, the evening, sleeps so peacefully!
Smoothed by long fingers,
Asleep... tired... or it malingers.
Stretched on the floor, here beside you and me.
Should I, after tea and cakes and ices,
Have the strength to force the moment to its crisis?
But though I have wept and fasted, wept and prayed,
Though I have seen my head (grown slightly bald) brought in upon a platter,
I am no prophet—and here's no great matter;
I have seen the moment of my greatness flicker,
And I have seen the eternal Footman hold my coat, and snicker,
And in short, I was afraid.

And would it have been worth it, after all,
After the cups, the marmalade, the tea,
Among the porcelain, among some talk of you and me,
Would it have been worth while,
To have bitten off the matter with a smile,
To have squeezed the universe into a ball
To roll it toward some overwhelming question,
To say: "I am Lazarus, come from the dead,
Come back to tell you all, I shall tell you all"—
If one, settling a pillow by her head,
  Should say: "That is not what I meant at all;
  That is not it, at all."

And would it have been worth it, after all,
Would it have been worth while,

After the sunsets and the dooryards and the sprinkled streets,
After the novels, after the teacups, after the skirts that trail along the
floor—
And this, and so much more?—
It is impossible to say just what I mean!
But as if a magic lantern threw the nerves in patterns on a screen:
Would it have been worth while
If one, settling a pillow or throwing off a shawl,
And turning toward the window, should say:
"That is not it at all,
That is not what I meant, at all."

. . . .

No! I am not Prince Hamlet, nor was meant to be;
Am an attendant lord, one that will do
To swell a progress, start a scene or two,
Advise the prince; no doubt, an easy tool,
Deferential, glad to be of use,
Politic, cautious, and meticulous;
Full of high sentence, but a bit obtuse;
At times, indeed, almost ridiculous—
Almost, at times, the Fool.

I grow old... I grow old...
I shall wear the bottoms of my trousers rolled.

Shall I part my hair behind? Do I dare to eat a peach?
I shall wear white flannel trousers, and walk upon the beach.
I have heard the mermaids singing, each to each.

I do not think that they will sing to me.

I have seen them riding seaward on the waves
Combing the white hair of the waves blown back
When the wind blows the water white and black.

We have lingered in the chambers of the sea
By sea-girls wreathed with seaweed red and brown
Till human voices wake us, and we drown.

Portrait of a Lady

Thou hast committed—
Fornication: but that was in another country
And besides, the wench is dead.
-The Jew of Malta.

I

Among the smoke and fog of a December afternoon
You have the scene arrange itself—as it will seem to do—
With "I have saved this afternoon for you";
And four wax candles in the darkened room,
Four rings of light upon the ceiling overhead,
An atmosphere of Juliet's tomb
Prepared for all the things to be said, or left unsaid.
We have been, let us say, to hear the latest Pole
Transmit the Preludes, through his hair and finger-tips.
"So intimate, this Chopin, that I think his soul
Should be resurrected only among friends
Some two or three, who will not touch the bloom
That is rubbed and questioned in the concert room."
—And so the conversation slips
Among velleities and carefully caught regrets
Through attenuated tones of violins
Mingled with remote cornets
And begins.

"You do not know how much they mean to me, my friends,
And how, how rare and strange it is, to find
In a life composed so much, so much of odds and ends,
(For indeed I do not love it... you knew? you are not blind!
How keen you are!)
To find a friend who has these qualities,
Who has, and gives
Those qualities upon which friendship lives.
How much it means that I say this to you—
Without these friendships—life, what cauchemar!"
Among the windings of the violins
And the ariettes
Of cracked cornets
Inside my brain a dull tom-tom begins
Absurdly hammering a prelude of its own,
Capricious monotone
That is at least one definite "false note."
—Let us take the air, in a tobacco trance,
Admire the monuments
Discuss the late events,
Correct our watches by the public clocks.
Then sit for half an hour and drink our bocks.

II

Now that lilacs are in bloom
She has a bowl of lilacs in her room
And twists one in her fingers while she talks.
"Ah, my friend, you do not know, you do not know
What life is, you should hold it in your hands";
(Slowly twisting the lilac stalks)

"You let it flow from you, you let it flow,
And youth is cruel, and has no remorse
And smiles at situations which it cannot see."
I smile, of course,
And go on drinking tea.
"Yet with these April sunsets, that somehow recall
My buried life, and Paris in the Spring,
I feel immeasurably at peace, and find the world
To be wonderful and youthful, after all."

The voice returns like the insistent out-of-tune
Of a broken violin on an August afternoon:
"I am always sure that you understand
My feelings, always sure that you feel,
Sure that across the gulf you reach your hand.

You are invulnerable, you have no Achilles' heel.
You will go on, and when you have prevailed
You can say: at this point many a one has failed.

But what have I, but what have I, my friend,
To give you, what can you receive from me?
Only the friendship and the sympathy
Of one about to reach her journey's end.

I shall sit here, serving tea to friends...."

I take my hat: how can I make a cowardly amends
For what she has said to me?
You will see me any morning in the park
Reading the comics and the sporting page.

Particularly I remark An English countess goes upon the stage.
A Greek was murdered at a Polish dance,
Another bank defaulter has confessed.
I keep my countenance, I remain self-possessed
Except when a street piano, mechanical and tired
Reiterates some worn-out common song
With the smell of hyacinths across the garden
Recalling things that other people have desired.
Are these ideas right or wrong?

III

The October night comes down; returning as before
Except for a slight sensation of being ill at ease
I mount the stairs and turn the handle of the door
And feel as if I had mounted on my hands and knees.

"And so you are going abroad; and when do you return?
But that's a useless question.
You hardly know when you are coming back,
You will find so much to learn."
My smile falls heavily among the bric-à-brac.

"Perhaps you can write to me."
My self-possession flares up for a second;
This is as I had reckoned.

"I have been wondering frequently of late
(But our beginnings never know our ends!)
Why we have not developed into friends."
I feel like one who smiles, and turning shall remark

Suddenly, his expression in a glass.
My self-possession gutters; we are really in the dark.

"For everybody said so, all our friends,
They all were sure our feelings would relate
So closely! I myself can hardly understand.
We must leave it now to fate.
You will write, at any rate.
Perhaps it is not too late.
I shall sit here, serving tea to friends."

And I must borrow every changing shape
To find expression... dance, dance
Like a dancing bear,
Cry like a parrot, chatter like an ape.
Let us take the air, in a tobacco trance—
Well! and what if she should die some afternoon,
Afternoon grey and smoky, evening yellow and rose;
Should die and leave me sitting pen in hand
With the smoke coming down above the housetops;
Doubtful, for quite a while
Not knowing what to feel or if I understand
Or whether wise or foolish, tardy or too soon...
Would she not have the advantage, after all?
This music is successful with a "dying fall"
Now that we talk of dying—
And should I have the right to smile?

Preludes

I

The winter evening settles down
With smell of steaks in passageways.
Six o'clock.
The burnt-out ends of smoky days.
And now a gusty shower wraps
The grimy scraps
Of withered leaves about your feet
And newspapers from vacant lots;
The showers beat
On broken blinds and chimney-pots,
And at the corner of the street
A lonely cab-horse steams and stamps.
And then the lighting of the lamps.

II

The morning comes to consciousness
Of faint stale smells of beer
From the sawdust-trampled street
With all its muddy feet that press
To early coffee-stands.

With the other masquerades
That time resumes,
One thinks of all the hands
That are raising dingy shades
In a thousand furnished rooms.

III

You tossed a blanket from the bed,
You lay upon your back, and waited;
You dozed, and watched the night revealing
The thousand sordid images
Of which your soul was constituted;
They flickered against the ceiling.
And when all the world came back
And the light crept up between the shutters,
And you heard the sparrows in the gutters,
You had such a vision of the street
As the street hardly understands;
Sitting along the bed's edge, where
You curled the papers from your hair,
Or clasped the yellow soles of feet
In the palms of both soiled hands.

IV

His soul stretched tight across the skies
That fade behind a city block,
Or trampled by insistent feet
At four and five and six o'clock;
And short square fingers stuffing pipes,

And evening newspapers, and eyes
Assured of certain certainties,
The conscience of a blackened street
Impatient to assume the world.

I am moved by fancies that are curled
Around these images, and cling:
The notion of some infinitely gentle
Infinitely suffering thing.

Wipe your hand across your mouth, and laugh;
The worlds revolve like ancient women
Gathering fuel in vacant lots.

Rhapsody on a Windy Night

Twelve o'clock.
Along the reaches of the street
Held in a lunar synthesis,
Whispering lunar incantations
Disolve the floors of memory
And all its clear relations,
Its divisions and precisions,
Every street lamp that I pass
Beats like a fatalistic drum,
And through the spaces of the dark
Midnight shakes the memory
As a madman shakes a dead geranium.

Half-past one,
The street lamp sputtered,
The street lamp muttered,
The street lamp said,
"Regard that woman
Who hesitates toward you in the light of the door
Which opens on her like a grin.
You see the border of her dress
Is torn and stained with sand,
And you see the corner of her eye
Twists like a crooked pin."

The memory throws up high and dry
A crowd of twisted things;
A twisted branch upon the beach
Eaten smooth, and polished
As if the world gave up
The secret of its skeleton,
Stiff and white.
A broken spring in a factory yard,
Rust that clings to the form that the strength has left
Hard and curled and ready to snap.

Half-past two,
The street-lamp said,
"Remark the cat which flattens itself in the gutter,
Slips out its tongue
And devours a morsel of rancid butter."
So the hand of the child, automatic,
Slipped out and pocketed a toy that was running along
the quay.
I could see nothing behind that child's eye.
I have seen eyes in the street
Trying to peer through lighted shutters,
And a crab one afternoon in a pool,
An old crab with barnacles on his back,
Gripped the end of a stick which I held him.

Half-past three,
The lamp sputtered,
The lamp muttered in the dark.

The lamp hummed:
"Regard the moon,
La lune ne garde aucune rancune,
She winks a feeble eye,
She smiles into corners.
She smooths the hair of the grass.
The moon has lost her memory.
A washed-out smallpox cracks her face,
Her hand twists a paper rose,
That smells of dust and old Cologne,
She is alone With all the old nocturnal smells
That cross and cross across her brain.
The reminiscence comes
Of sunless dry geraniums
And dust in crevices,
Smells of chestnuts in the streets
And female smells in shuttered rooms
And cigarettes in corridors
And cocktail smells in bars."

The lamp said,
"Four o'clock,
Here is the number on the door.
Memory!
You have the key,
The little lamp spreads a ring on the stair,
Mount.
The bed is open; the tooth-brush hangs on the wall,
Put your shoes at the door, sleep, prepare for life."

The last twist of the knife.

Morning at the Window

They are rattling breakfast plates in basement kitchens,
And along the trampled edges of the street
I am aware of the damp souls of housemaids
Sprouting despondently at area gates.
The brown waves of fog toss up to me
Twisted faces from the bottom of the street,
And tear from a passer-by with muddy skirts
An aimless smile that hovers in the air
And vanishes along the level of the roofs.

The Boston Evening Transcript

The readers of the Boston Evening Transcript
Sway in the wind like a field of ripe corn.
When evening quickens faintly in the street,
Wakening the appetites of life in some
And to others bringing the Boston Evening Transcript,
I mount the steps and ring the bell, turning
Wearily, as one would turn to nod good-bye to Rochefoucauld,
If the street were time and he at the end of the street,
And I say, "Cousin Harriet, here is the Boston Evening Transcript."

Aunt Helen

Miss Helen Slingsby was my maiden aunt,
And lived in a small house near a fashionable square
Cared for by servants to the number of four.
Now when she died there was silence in heaven
And silence at her end of the street.
The shutters were drawn and the undertaker wiped his feet—
He was aware that this sort of thing had occurred before.
The dogs were handsomely provided for,
But shortly afterwards the parrot died too.
The Dresden clock continued ticking on the mantelpiece,
And the footman sat upon the dining-table
Holding the second housemaid on his knees—
Who had always been so careful while her mistress lived.

Cousin Nancy

Miss Nancy Ellicott Strode across the hills and broke them,
Rode across the hills and broke them—
The barren New England hills—
Riding to hounds
Over the cow-pasture.

Miss Nancy Ellicott smoked
And danced all the modern dances;
And her aunts were not quite sure how they felt about it,
But they knew that it was modern.

Upon the glazen shelves kept watch
Matthew and Waldo, guardians of the faith,
The army of unalterable law.

Mr. Apollinax

When Mr. Apollinax visited the United States
His laughter tinkled among the teacups.
I thought of Fragilion, that shy figure among the birch-trees,
And of Priapus in the shrubbery
Gaping at the lady in the swing.
In the palace of Mrs. Phlaccus, at Professor Channing-Cheetah's
He laughed like an irresponsible foetus.
His laughter was submarine and profound
Like the old man of the sea's
Hidden under coral islands
Where worried bodies of drowned men drift down in the green silence,
Dropping from fingers of surf.
I looked for the head of Mr. Apollinax rolling under a chair
Or grinning over a screen
With seaweed in its hair.
I heard the beat of centaur's hoofs over the hard turf
As his dry and passionate talk devoured the afternoon.
"He is a charming man"—"But after all what did he mean?"—
"His pointed ears... He must be unbalanced,"—
"There was something he said that I might have challenged."
Of dowager Mrs. Phlaccus, and Professor and Mrs. Cheetah
I remember a slice of lemon, and a bitten macaroon.

Hysteria

As she laughed I was aware of becoming involved in her laughter and being part of it, until her teeth were only accidental stars with a talent for squad-drill. I was drawn in by short gasps, inhaled at each momentary recovery, lost finally in the dark caverns of her throat, bruised by the ripple of unseen muscles. An elderly waiter with trembling hands was hurriedly spreading a pink and white checked cloth over the rusty green iron table, saying: "If the lady and gentleman wish to take their tea in the garden, if the lady and gentleman wish to take their tea in the garden..." I decided that if the shaking of her breasts could be stopped, some of the fragments of the afternoon might be collected, and I concentrated my attention with careful subtlety to this end.

Conversation Galante

I observe: "Our sentimental friend the moon!
Or possibly (fantastic, I confess)
It may be Prester John's balloon
Or an old battered lantern hung aloft
To light poor travellers to their distress."
  She then: "How you digress!"

And I then: "Some one frames upon the keys
That exquisite nocturne, with which we explain
The night and moonshine; music which we seize
To body forth our vacuity."
  She then: "Does this refer to me?"
  "Oh no, it is I who am inane."

"You, madam, are the eternal humorist,
The eternal enemy of the absolute,
Giving our vagrant moods the slightest twist!
With your air indifferent and imperious
At a stroke our mad poetics to confute—"
  And—"Are we then so serious?"

La Figlia Che Piange

O quam te memorem Virgo...

Stand on the highest pavement of the stair—
Lean on a garden urn—
Weave, weave the sunlight in your hair—
Clasp your flowers to you with a pained surprise—
Fling them to the ground and turn
With a fugitive resentment in your eyes:
But weave, weave the sunlight in your hair.

So I would have had him leave,
So I would have had her stand and grieve,
So he would have left
As the soul leaves the body torn and bruised,
As the mind deserts the body it has used.
I should find
Some way incomparably light and deft,
Some way we both should understand,
Simple and faithless as a smile and shake of the hand.

She turned away, but with the autumn weather
Compelled my imagination many days,
Many days and many hours:
Her hair over her arms and her arms full of flowers.
And I wonder how they should have been together!
I should have lost a gesture and a pose.
Sometimes these cogitations still amaze
The troubled midnight and the noon's repose.

EELDROP AND APPLEPLEX

I

Eeldrop and Appleplex rented two small rooms in a disreputable part of town. Here they sometimes came at nightfall, here they sometimes slept, and after they had slept, they cooked oatmeal and departed in the morning for destinations unknown to each other. They sometimes slept, more often they talked, or looked out of the window.

They had chosen the rooms and the neighborhood with great care. There are evil neighborhoods of noise and evil neighborhoods of silence, and Eeldrop and Appleplex preferred the latter, as being the more evil. It was a shady street, its windows were heavily curtained; and over it hung the cloud of a respectability which has something to conceal. Yet it had the advantage of more riotous neighborhoods near by, and Eeldrop and Appleplex commanded from their windows the entrance of a police station across the way. This alone possessed an irresistible appeal in their eyes. From time to time the silence of the street was broken; whenever a malefactor was apprehended, a wave of excitement curled into the street and broke upon the doors of the police station. Then the inhabitants of the street would linger in dressing-gowns, upon their doorsteps: then alien visitors would linger in the street, in caps; long after the centre of misery had been engulphed in his cell. Then Eeldrop and Appleplex would break off their discourse, and rush out to mingle with the mob. Each pursued his own line of enquiry. Appleplex, who had the gift of an extraordinary address with the lower classes of both sexes, questioned the onlookers, and usually extracted full and inconsistent histories: Eeldrop preserved a more passive demeanor, listened to the conversation of the people among themselves, registered in his mind their oaths, their redundance of phrase, their various manners of spitting, and the cries of the victim from the hall of justice within. When the crowd dispersed, Eeldrop and Appleplex returned to their rooms: Appleplex entered the results of his inquiries into large notebooks, filed according to the nature of the case, from A (adultery) to Y (yeggmen). Eeldrop smoked reflectively. It may be added that Eeldrop was a sceptic, with a taste for mysticism, and Appleplex a materialist with a leaning toward scepticism; that Eeldrop was learned in theology, and that Appleplex studied the physical and biological sciences.

There was a common motive which led Eeldrop and Appleplex thus to separate themselves from time to time, from the fields of their daily employments and their ordinarily social activities. Both were endeavoring to escape not the commonplace, respectable or even the domestic, but the too well pigeonholed, too taken-for-granted, too highly systematized areas, and,—in the language of those whom they sought to avoid—they wished "to apprehend the human soul in its concrete individuality."

"Why," said Eeldrop, "was that fat Spaniard, who sat at the table with us this evening, and listened to our conversation with occasional curiosity, why was he himself for a moment an object of interest to us? He wore his napkin tucked into his chin, he made unpleasant noises while eating, and while not eating, his way of crumbling bread between fat fingers made me extremely nervous: he wore a waistcoat cafe au lait, and black boots with brown tops. He was oppressively gross and vulgar; he belonged to a type, he could easily be classified in any town of provincial Spain. Yet under the circumstances—when we had been discussing marriage, and he suddenly leaned forward and exclaimed: 'I was married once myself'—we were able to detach him from his classification and regard him for a moment as an unique being, a soul, however insignificant, with a history of its own, once for all. It is these moments which we prize, and which alone are revealing. For any vital truth is incapable of being applied to another case: the essential is unique. Perhaps that is why it is so neglected: because it is useless. What we learned about that Spaniard is incapable of being applied to any other Spaniard, or even recalled in words. With the decline of orthodox theology and its admirable theory of the soul, the unique importance of events has vanished. A man is only important as he is classed. Hence there is no tragedy, or no appreciation of tragedy, which is the same thing. We had been talking of young Bistwick, who three months ago married his mother's housemaid and now is aware of the fact. Who appreciates the truth of the matter? Not the relatives, for they are only moved by affection, by regard for Bistwick's interests, and chiefly by their collective feeling of family disgrace. Not the generous minded and thoughtful outsider, who regards it merely as evidence for the necessity of divorce law reform. Bistwick is classed among the unhappily married. But what Bistwick feels when he wakes up in the morning, which is the great important fact, no detached outsider conceives. The awful importance of the ruin of a life is overlooked. Men are only allowed to be happy or miserable in classes. In Gopsum Street a man murders his mistress. The important fact is that for the man the act is eternal, and that for the brief space he has to live, he is already dead. He is already in a different world from ours. He has crossed the frontier. The important fact is that something is done which can not be undone—a possibility which none of us realize until we face it ourselves. For the man's neighbors the important fact is what the man killed her with? And at precisely what time? And who found the body? For the 'enlightened public' the case is merely evidence for the Drink question, or Unemployment, or some other category of things to be reformed. But the mediaeval world, insisting on the eternity of punishment, expressed something nearer the truth."

"What you say," replied Appleplex, "commands my measured adherence. I should think, in the case of the Spaniard, and in the many other interesting cases which have come under our attention at the door of the police station, what we grasp in that moment of pure observation on which we pride ourselves, is not alien to the principle of classification, but deeper. We could, if we liked, make excellent comment upon the nature of provincial Spaniards, or of destitution (as misery is called by the philanthropists), or on homes for working girls. But such is not our intention. We aim at experience in the particular centres in which alone it is evil. We avoid classification. We do not deny it. But when a man is classified something is lost. The majority of mankind live on paper currency: they use terms which are merely good for so much reality, they never see actual coinage."

"I should go even further than that," said Eeldrop. "The majority not only have no language to express anything save generalized man; they are for the most part unaware of themselves as anything but generalized men. They are first of all government officials, or pillars of the church, or trade unionists, or poets, or unemployed; this cataloguing is not only satisfactory to other people for practical purposes, it is sufficient to themselves for their 'life of the spirit.' Many are not quite real at any moment. When Wolstrip married, I am sure he said to himself: 'Now I am consummating the union of two of the best families in Philadelphia.'"

"The question is," said Appleplex, "what is to be our philosophy. This must be settled at once. Mrs. Howexden recommends me to read Bergson. He writes very entertainingly on the structure of the eye of the frog."

"Not at all," interrupted his friend. "Our philosophy is quite irrelevant. The essential is, that our philosophy should spring from our point of view and not return upon itself to explain our point of view. A philosophy about intuition is somewhat less likely to be intuitive than any other. We must avoid having a platform."

"But at least," said Appleplex, "we are..."

"Individualists. No!! nor anti-intellectualists. These also are labels. The 'individualist' is a member of a mob as fully as any other man: and the mob of individualists is the most unpleasing, because it has the least character. Nietzsche was a mob-man, just as Bergson is an intellectualist. We cannot escape the label, but let it be one which carries no distinction, and arouses no self-consciousness. Sufficient that we should find simple labels, and not further exploit them. I am, I confess to you, in private life, a bank-clerk...."

"And should, according to your own view, have a wife, three children, and a vegetable garden in a suburb," said Appleplex.

"Such is precisely the case," returned Eeldrop, "but I had not thought it necessary to mention this biographical detail. As it is Saturday night, I shall return to my suburb. Tomorrow will be spent in that garden...."

"I shall pay my call on Mrs. Howexden," murmured Appleplex.

II

The suburban evening was grey and yellow on Sunday; the gardens of the small houses to left and right were rank with ivy and tall grass and lilac bushes; the tropical South London verdure was dusty above and mouldy below; the tepid air swarmed with flies. Eeldrop, at the window, welcomed the smoky smell of lilac, the gramaphones, the choir of the Baptist chapel, and the sight of three small girls playing cards on the steps of the police station.

"On such a night as this," said Eeldrop, "I often think of Scheherazade, and wonder what has become of her."

Appleplex rose without speaking and turned to the files which contained the documents for his "Survey of Contemporary Society." He removed the file marked London from between the files Barcelona and Boston where it had been misplaced, and turned over the papers rapidly. "The lady you mention," he rejoined at last, "whom I have listed not under S. but as Edith, alias Scheherazade, has left but few evidences in my possession. Here is an old laundry account which she left for you to pay, a cheque drawn by her and marked 'R/D,' a letter from her mother in Honolulu (on ruled paper), a poem written on a restaurant bill—'To Atthis'—and a letter by herself, on Lady Equistep's best notepaper, containing some damaging but entertaining information about Lady Equistep. Then there are my own few observations on two sheets of foolscap."

"Edith," murmured Eeldrop, who had not been attending to this catalogue, "I wonder what has become of her. 'Not pleasure, but fulness of life... to burn ever with a hard gem-like flame,' those were her words. What curiosity and passion for experience! Perhaps that flame has burnt itself out by now."

"You ought to inform yourself better," said Appleplex severely, "Edith dines sometimes with Mrs. Howexden, who tells me that her passion for experience has taken her to a Russian pianist in Bayswater. She is also said to be present often at the Anarchist Tea Rooms, and can usually be found in the evening at the Cafe de l'Orangerie."

"Well," replied Eeldrop, "I confess that I prefer to wonder what has become of her. I do not like to think of her future. Scheherazade grown old! I see her grown very plump, full-bosomed, with blond hair, living in a small flat with a maid, walking in the Park with a Pekinese, motoring with a Jewish stock-broker. With a fierce appetite for food and drink, when all other appetite is gone, all other appetite gone except the insatiable increasing appetite of vanity; rolling on two wide legs, rolling in motorcars, rolling toward a diabetic end in a seaside watering place."

"Just now you saw that bright flame burning itself out," said Appleplex, "now you see it guttering thickly, which proves that your vision was founded on imagination, not on feeling. And the passion for experience—have you remained so impregnably Pre-Raphaelite as to believe in that? What real person, with the genuine resources of instinct, has ever believed in the passion for experience? The passion for experience is a criticism of the sincere, a creed only of the histrionic. The passionate person is passionate about this or that, perhaps about the least significant things, but not about experience. But Marius, des Esseintes, Edith..."

"But consider," said Eeldrop, attentive only to the facts of Edith's history, and perhaps missing the point of Appleplex's remarks, "her unusual career. The daughter of a piano tuner in Honolulu, she secured a scholarship at the University of California, where she graduated with Honors in Social Ethics. She then married a celebrated billiard professional in San Francisco, after an acquaintance of twelve hours, lived with him for two days, joined a musical comedy chorus, and was divorced in Nevada. She turned up several years later in Paris and was known to all the Americans and English at the Cafe du Dome as Mrs. Short. She reappeared in London as Mrs. Griffiths, published a small volume of verse, and was accepted in several circles known to us. And now, as I still insist, she has disappeared from society altogether."

"The memory of Scheherazade," said Appleplex, "is to me that of Bird's custard and prunes in a Bloomsbury boarding house. It is not my intention to represent Edith as merely disreputable. Neither is she a tragic figure. I want to know why she misses. I cannot altogether analyse her 'into a combination of known elements' but I fail to touch anything definitely unanalysable.

"Is Edith, in spite of her romantic past, pursuing steadily some hidden purpose of her own? Are her migrations and eccentricities the sign of some unguessed consistency? I find in her a quantity of shrewd observation, an excellent fund of criticism, but I cannot connect them into any peculiar vision. Her sarcasm at the expense of her friends is delightful, but I doubt whether it is more than an attempt to mould herself from outside, by the impact of hostilities, to emphasise her isolation. Everyone says of her, 'How perfectly impenetrable!' I suspect that within there is only the confusion of a dusty garret."

"I test people," said Eeldrop, "by the way in which I imagine them as waking up in the morning. I am not drawing upon memory when I imagine Edith waking to a room strewn with clothes, papers, cosmetics, letters and a few books, the smell of Violettes de Parme and stale tobacco. The sunlight beating in through broken blinds, and broken blinds keeping out the sun until Edith can compel herself to attend to another day. Yet the vision does not give me much pain. I think of her as an artist without the slightest artistic power."

"The artistic temperament—" began Appleplex.

"No, not that." Eeldrop snatched away the opportunity. "I mean that what holds the artist together is the work which he does; separate him from his work and he either disintegrates or solidifies. There is no interest in the artist apart from his work. And there are, as you said, those people who provide material for the artist. Now Edith's poem 'To Atthis' proves beyond the shadow of a doubt that she is not an artist. On the other hand I have often thought of her, as I thought this evening, as presenting possibilities for poetic purposes. But the people who can be material for art must have in them something unconscious, something which they do not fully realise or understand. Edith, in spite of what is called her impenetrable mask, presents herself too well. I cannot use her; she uses herself too fully. Partly for the same reason I think, she fails to be an artist: she does not live at all upon instinct. The artist is part of him a drifter, at the mercy of impressions, and another part of him allows this to happen for the sake of making use of the unhappy creature. But in Edith the division is merely the rational, the cold and detached part of the artist, itself divided. Her material, her experience that is, is already a mental product, already digested by reason. Hence Edith (I only at this moment arrive at understanding) is really the most orderly person in existence, and the most rational. Nothing ever happens to her; everything that happens is her own doing."

"And hence also," continued Appleplex, catching up the thread, "Edith is the least detached of all persons, since to be detached is to be detached from one's self, to stand by and criticise coldly one's own passions and vicissitudes. But in Edith the critic is coaching the combatant."

"Edith is not unhappy."

"She is dissatisfied, perhaps."

"But again I say, she is not tragic: she is too rational. And in her career there is no progression, no decline or degeneration. Her condition is once and for always. There is and will be no catastrophe.

"But I am tired. I still wonder what Edith and Mrs. Howexden have in common. This invites the consideration (you may not perceive the connection) of Sets and Society, a subject which we can pursue tomorrow night."

Appleplex looked a little embarrassed. "I am dining with Mrs. Howexden," he said. "But I will reflect upon the topic before I see you again."

EZRA POUND: HIS METRIC AND POETRY

I

"All talk on modern poetry, by people who know," wrote Mr. Carl Sandburg in *Poetry*, "ends with dragging in Ezra Pound somewhere. He may be named only to be cursed as wanton and mocker, poseur, trifler and vagrant. Or he may be classed as filling a niche today like that of Keats in a preceding epoch. The point is, he will be mentioned."

This is a simple statement of fact. But though Mr. Pound is well known, even having been the victim of interviews for Sunday papers, it does not follow that his work is thoroughly known. There are twenty people who have their opinion of him for every one who has read his writings with any care. Of those twenty, there will be some who are shocked, some who are ruffled, some who are irritated, and one or two whose sense of dignity is outraged. The twenty-first critic will probably be one who knows and admires some of the poems, but who either says: "Pound is primarily a scholar, a translator," or "Pound's early verse was beautiful; his later work shows nothing better than the itch for advertisement, a mischievous desire to be annoying, or a childish desire to be original." There is a third type of reader, rare enough, who has perceived Mr. Pound for some years, who has followed his career intelligently, and who recognizes its consistency.

This essay is not written for the first twenty critics of literature, nor for that rare twenty-second who has just been mentioned, but for the admirer of a poem here or there, whose appreciation is capable of yielding him a larger return. If the reader is already at the stage where he can maintain at once the two propositions, "Pound is merely a scholar" and "Pound is merely a yellow journalist," or the other two propositions, "Pound is merely a technician" and "Pound is merely a prophet of chaos," then there is very little hope. But there are readers of poetry who have not yet reached this hypertrophy of the logical faculty; their attention might be arrested, not by an outburst of praise, but by a simple statement. The present essay aims merely at such a statement. It is not intended to be either a biographical or a critical study. It will not dilate upon "beauties"; it is a summary account of ten years' work in poetry. The citations from reviews will perhaps stimulate the reader to form his own opinion. We do not wish to form it for him. Nor shall we enter into other phases of Mr. Pound's activity during this ten years; his writings and views on art and music; though these would take an important place in any comprehensive biography.

II

Pound's first book was published in Venice. Venice was a halting point after he had left America and before he had settled in England, and here, in 1908, "A Lume Spento" appeared. The volume is now a rarity of literature; it was published by the author and made at a Venetian press where the author was able personally to supervise the printing; on paper which was a remainder of a supply which had been used for a History of the Church. Pound left Venice in the same year, and took "A Lume Spento" with him to London. It was not to be expected that a first book of verse, published by an unknown American in Venice, should attract much attention. The "Evening Standard" has the distinction of having noticed the volume, in a review summing it up as:

> wild and haunting stuff, absolutely poetic, original, imaginative, passionate, and spiritual. Those who do not consider it crazy may well consider it inspired. Coming after the trite and decorous verse of most of our decorous poets, this poet seems like a minstrel of Provençe at a suburban musical evening.... The unseizable magic of poetry is in the queer paper volume, and words are no good in describing it.

As the chief poems in "A Lume Spento" were afterwards incorporated in "Personae," the book demands mention only as a date in the author's history. "Personae," the first book published in London, followed early in 1909. Few poets have undertaken the siege of London with so little backing; few books of verse have ever owed their success so purely to their own merits. Pound came to London a complete stranger, without either literary patronage or financial means. He took "Personae" to Mr. Elkin Mathews, who has the glory of having published Yeats' "Wind Among the Reeds," and the "Books of the Rhymers' Club," in which many of the poets of the '90s, now famous, found a place. Mr. Mathews first suggested, as was natural to an unknown author, that the author should bear part of the cost of printing. "I have a shilling in my pocket, if that is any use to you," said the latter. "Well," said Mr. Mathews, "I want to publish it anyway." His acumen was justified. The book was, it is true, received with opposition, but it was received. There were a few appreciative critics, notably Mr. Edward Thomas, the poet (known also as "Edward Eastaway"; he has since been killed in France). Thomas, writing in the "English Review" (then in its brightest days under the editorship of Ford Madox Hueffer), recognized the first-hand intensity of feeling in "Personae":

> He has ... hardly any of the superficial good qualities of modern versifiers.... He has not the current melancholy or resignation or unwillingness to live; nor the kind of feeling for nature which runs to minute description and decorative metaphor. He cannot be usefully compared with any living writers;... full of personality and with such power to express it, that from the first to the last lines of most of his poems he holds us steadily in his own pure grave, passionate world.... The beauty of it (In Praise of Ysolt) is the beauty of passion, sincerity and intensity, not of

beautiful words and images and suggestions ... the thought dominates the words and is greater than they are. Here (Idyll for Glaucus) the effect is full of human passion and natural magic, without any of the phrases which a reader of modern verse would expect in the treatment of such a subject.

Mr. Scott James, in the "Daily News," speaks in praise of his metres:

At first the whole thing may seem to be mere madness and rhetoric, a vain exhibition of force and passion without beauty. But, as we read on, these curious metres of his seem to have a law and order of their own; the brute force of Mr. Pound's imagination seems to impart some quality of infectious beauty to his words. Sometimes there is a strange beating of anapaests when he quickens to his subject; again and again he unexpectedly ends a line with the second half of a reverberant hexameter:

"Flesh shrouded, bearing the secret."

... And a few lines later comes an example of his favourite use of spondee, followed by dactyl and spondee, which comes in strangely and, as we first read it, with the appearance of discord, but afterwards seems to gain a curious and distinctive vigour:

"Eyes, dreams, lips, and the night goes."

Another line like the end of a hexameter is

"But if e'er I come to my love's land."

But even so favourable a critic pauses to remark that

> He baffles us by archaic words and unfamiliar metres; he often seems to be scorning the limitations of form and metre, breaking out into any sort of expression which suits itself to his mood.

and counsels the poet to "have a little more respect for his art."

It is, in fact, just this adaptability of metre to mood, an adaptability due to an intensive study of metre, that constitutes an important element in Pound's technique. Few readers were prepared to accept or follow the amount of erudition which entered into "Personae" and its close successor, "Exultations," or to devote the care to reading them which they demand. It is here that many have been led astray. Pound is not one of those poets who make no demand of the reader; and the casual reader of verse, disconcerted by the difference between Pound's poetry and that on which his taste has been trained, attributes his own difficulties to excessive scholarship on the part of the author. "This," he will say of some of the poems in Provençal form or on Provençal subjects, "is archaeology; it requires knowledge on the part of its reader, and true poetry does not require such knowledge." But to display knowledge is not the same thing as to expect it on the part of the reader; and of this sort of pedantry Pound is quite free. He is, it is true, one of the most learned of poets. In America he had taken up the study of Romance Languages with the intention of teaching. After work in Spain and Italy, after pursuing the Provençal verb from Milan to Freiburg, he deserted the thesis on Lope de Vega and the Ph.D. and the professorial chair, and elected to remain in Europe. Mr. Pound has spoken out his mind from time to time on the subject of scholarship in American universities, its deadness, its isolation from genuine appreciation, and the active creative life of literature. He has always been ready to battle against pedantry. As for his own learning, he has studied poetry carefully, and has made use of his study in his own verse. "Personae" and "Exultations" show his talent for turning his studies to account. He was supersaturated in Provençe; he had tramped over most of the country; and the life of the courts where the Troubadours thronged was part of his own life to him. Yet, though "Personae" and "Exultations" do exact something from the reader, they do not require a knowledge of Provençal or of Spanish or Italian. Very few people know the Arthurian legends well, or even Malory (if they did they might realize that the Idylls of the King are hardly more important than a parody, or a "Chaucer retold for Children"); but no one accuses Tennyson of needing footnotes, or of superciliousness toward the uninstructed. The difference is merely in what people are prepared for; most readers could no more relate the myth of Atys correctly than they could give a biography of Bertrand de Born. It is hardly too much to say that there is no poem in these volumes of Mr. Pound which needs fuller explanation than he gives himself. What the poems do require is a trained ear, or at least the willingness to be trained.

The metres and the use of language are unfamiliar. There are certain traces of modern influence. We cannot agree with Mr. Scott-James that among these are "W. E. Henley, Kipling, Chatterton, and especially Walt Whitman"—least of all Walt Whitman. Probably there are only two: Yeats and Browning. Yeats in "La Fraisne," in "Personae," for instance, in the attitude and somewhat in the vocabulary:

I wrapped my tears in an ellum leaf
And left them under a stone,
And now men call me mad because I have thrown
All folly from me, putting it aside

To leave the old barren ways of men ...

For Browning, Mr. Pound has always professed strong admiration (see "Mesmerism" in "Personae"); there are traces of him in "Cino" and "Famam Librosque Cano," in the same volume. But it is more profitable to comment upon the variety of metres and the original use of language.

Ezra Pound has been fathered with vers libre in English, with all its vices and virtues. The term is a loose one—any verse is called "free" by people whose ears are not accustomed to it—in the second place, Pound's use of this medium has shown the temperance of the artist, and his belief in it as a vehicle is not that of the fanatic. He has said himself that when one has the proper material for a sonnet, one should use the sonnet form; but that it happens very rarely to any poet to find himself in possession of just the block of stuff which can perfectly be modelled into the sonnet. It is true that up to very recently it was impossible to get free verse printed in any periodical except those in which Pound had influence; and that now it is possible to print free verse (second, third, or tenth-rate) in almost any American magazine. Who is responsible for the bad free verse is a question of no importance, inasmuch as its authors would have written bad verse in any form; Pound has at least the right to be judged by the success or failure of his own. Pound's vers libre is such as is only possible for a poet who has worked tirelessly with rigid forms and different systems of metric. His "Canzoni" are in a way aside from his direct line of progress; they are much more nearly studies in mediaeval appreciation than any of his other verse; but they are interesting, apart from their merit, as showing the poet at work with the most intricate Provençal forms—so intricate that the pattern cannot be exhibited without quoting an entire poem. (M. Jean de Bosschere, whose French is translated in the "Egoist," has already called attention to the fact that Pound was the first writer in English to use five Provençal forms.) Quotation will show, however, the great variety of rhythm which Pound manages to introduce into the ordinary iambic pentameter:

Thy gracious ways,
O lady of my heart, have
O'er all my thought their golden glamour cast;
As amber torch-flames, where strange men-at-arms
Tread softly 'neath the damask shield of night,
Rise from the flowing steel in part reflected,
So on my mailed thought that with thee goeth,
Though dark the way, a golden glamour falleth.

Within the iambic limits, there are no two lines in the whole poem that have an identical rhythm.

We turn from this to a poem in "Exultations," the "Night Litany":

O God, what great kindness
have we done in times past
and forgotten it,
That thou givest this wonder unto us,
O God of waters?

O God of the night
What great sorrow
Cometh unto us,
That thou thus repayest us
Before the time of its coming?

There is evident, and more strongly in certain later poems, a tendency toward quantitative measure. Such a "freedom" as this lays so heavy a burden upon every word in a line that it becomes impossible to write like Shelley, leaving blanks for the adjectives, or like Swinburne, whose adjectives are practically blanks. Other poets have manipulated a great variety of metres and forms; but few have studied the forms and metres which they use so carefully as has Pound. His ballad of the "Goodly Fere" shows great knowledge of the ballad form:

I ha' seen him cow a thousand men
On the hills o' Galilee,
They whined as he walked out calm between
Wi' his eyes like the grey o' the sea.

Like the sea that brooks no voyaging
With the winds unleashed and free,
Like the sea that he cowed at Genseret
Wi' twey words spoke suddently.

A master of men was the Goodly Fere
A mate of the wind and sea,
If they think they ha' slain our Goodly Fere
They are fools eternally.

I ha' seen him eat o' the honey-comb
Sin' they nailed him to the tree.

And from this we turn to a very different form in the "Altaforte," which is perhaps the best sestina that has been written in English:

Damn it all! all this our South stinks peace.
You whoreson dog, Papiols, come! let's to music!
I have no life save when the swords clash.
But ah! when I see the standards gold, vair, purple, opposing,
And the broad fields beneath them turn crimson,
Then howl I my heart nigh mad with rejoicing.

In hot summer have I great rejoicing
When the tempests kill the earth's foul peace,
And the lightnings from black heaven flash crimson,
And the fierce thunders roar me their music
And the winds shriek through the clouds mad, opposing,
And through all the riven skies God's swords clash.

I have quoted two verses to show the intricacy of the pattern.

The Provençal canzon, like the Elizabethan lyric, was written for music. Mr. Pound has more recently insisted, in a series of articles on the work of Arnold Dolmetsch, in the "Egoist," on the importance of a study of music for the poet.

Such a relation between poetry and music is very different from what is called the "music" of Shelley or Swinburne, a music often nearer to rhetoric (or the art of the orator) than to the instrument. For poetry to approach the condition of music (Pound quotes approvingly the dictum of Pater) it is not necessary that poetry should be destitute of meaning. Instead of slightly veiled and resonant abstractions, like

Time with a gift of tears,
Grief with a glass that ran—

of Swinburne, or the mossiness of Mallarmé, Pound's verse is always definite and concrete, because he has always a definite emotion behind it.

Though I've roamed through many places,
None there is that my heart troweth
Fair as that wherein fair groweth
One whose laud here interlaces
Tuneful words, that I've essayed.

Let this tune be gently played
Which my voice herward upraises.

At the end of this poem the author appends the note:

> The form and measure are those of Piere Vidal's "*Ab l'alen tir vas me l'aire.*" The song is fit only to be sung, and is not to be spoken.

There are, here and there, deliberate archaisms or oddities (e.g., "herward"); there are deliberately arbitrary images, having their place in the total effect of the poem:

Red leaf that art blown upward and out and over
The green sheaf of the world ...

The lotos that pours
Her fragrance into the purple cup ...

Black lightning ... (in a more recent poem)

but no word is ever chosen merely for the tinkle; each has always its part in producing an impression which is produced always through language. Words are perhaps the hardest of all material of art: for they must be used to express both visual beauty and beauty of sound, as well as communicating a grammatical statement. It would be interesting to compare Pound's use of images with Mallarmé's; I think it will be found that the former's, by the contrast, will appear always sharp in outline, even if arbitrary and not photographic. Such images as those quoted above are as precise in their way as

Sur le Noel, morte saison,
Lorsque les loups vivent de vent ...

and the rest of that memorable Testament.

So much for the imagery. As to the "freedom" of his verse, Pound has made several statements in his articles on Dolmetsch which are to the point:

> Any work of art is a compound of freedom and order. It is perfectly obvious that art hangs between chaos on the one side and mechanics on the other. A pedantic insistence upon detail tends to drive out "major form." A firm hold on major form makes for a freedom of detail. In painting men intent on minutiae gradually lost the sense of form and form-combination. An attempt to restore this sense is branded as "revolution." It is revolution in the philological sense of the term....
>
> Art is a departure from fixed positions; felicitous departure from a norm....

The freedom of Pound's verse is rather a state of tension due to constant opposition between free and strict. There are not, as a matter of fact, two kinds of verse, the strict and the free; there is only a mastery which comes of being so well trained that form is an instinct and can be adapted to the particular purpose in hand.

After "Exultations" came the translation of the "Sonnets and Ballate of Guido Cavalcanti." It is worth noting that the writer of a long review in the "*Quest*"—speaking in praise of the translation, yet found fault with the author not on the ground of excessive mediaevalism, but because

> he is concerned rather with the future than with a somewhat remote past, so that in spite of his love for the mediaeval poets, his very accomplishment as a distinctly modern poet

> makes against his success as a wholly acceptable translator
> of Cavalcanti, the heir of the Troubadours, the scholastic.

Yet the *Daily News*, in criticising "Canzoni," had remarked that Mr. Pound

> seems to us rather a scholar than a poet, and we should like
> to see him giving his unusual talent more to direct
> translation from the Provençal.

and Mr. J. C. Squire (now the literary editor of the *New Statesman*), in an appreciative review in the *New Age*, had counselled the poet that he would

> gain and not lose if he could forget all about the poets of
> Dante's day, their roses and their flames, their gold and
> their falcons, and their literary amorousness, and walk out
> of the library into the fresh air.

In "Ripostes" there are traces of a different idiom. Superficially, the work may appear less important. The diction is more restrained, the flights shorter, the dexterity of technique is less arresting. By romantic readers the book would be considered less "passionate." But there is a much more solid substratum to this book; there is more thought; greater depth, if less agitation on the surface. The effect of London is apparent; the author has become a critic of men, surveying them from a consistent and developed point of view; he is more formidable and disconcerting; in short, much more mature. That he abandons nothing of his technical skill is evident from the translation from the Anglo-Saxon, the "Seafarer." It is not a slight achievement to have brought to life alliterative verse: perhaps the "Seafarer" is the only successful piece of alliterative verse ever written in modern English; alliterative verse which is not merely a clever tour de force, but which suggests the possibility of a new development of this form. Mr. Richard Aldington (whose own accomplishments as a writer of vers libre qualify him to speak) called the poem "unsurpassed and unsurpassable," and a writer in the *New Age* (a literary organ which has always been strongly opposed to metrical innovations) called it "one of the finest literary works of art produced in England during the last ten years." And the rough, stern beauty of the Anglo-Saxon, we may remark, is at the opposite pole from that of the Provençal and Italian poets to whom Pound had previously devoted his attention.

May I for my own self song's truth reckon,
Journey's jargon, how I in harsh days
Hardship endured oft.

But we can notice in "Ripostes" other evidences than of versatility only; certain poems show Mr. Pound turning to more modern subjects, as in the "Portrait d'une femme," or the mordant epigram, "An Object." Many readers are apt to confuse the maturing of personality with desiccation of the emotions. There is no desiccation in "Ripostes." This should be evident to anyone who reads carefully such a poem as "A Girl." We quote it entire without comment.

The tree has entered my hands,
The sap has ascended my arms,
The tree has grown in my breast—
Downward,
The branches grow out of me, like arms.

Tree you are,
Moss you are,
You are violets with wind above them.

A child—*so* high—you are,
And all this is folly to the world.

"The Return" is an important study in verse which is really quantitative. We quote only a few lines:

See, they return; ah, see the tentative
Movements, and the slow feet,
The trouble in the pace and the uncertain
Wavering!

"Ripostes" belongs to the period when Mr. Pound was being attacked because of his propaganda. He became known as the inventor of "Imagism," and later, as the "High Priest of Vorticism." As a matter of fact, the actual "propaganda" of Mr. Pound has been very small in quantity. The impression which his personality made, however, is suggested by the following note in "*Punch*," which is always a pretty reliable barometer of the English middle-class Grin:

> Mr. Welkin Mark (exactly opposite Long Jane's) begs to announce that he has secured for the English market the palpitating works of the new Montana (U.S.A.) poet, Mr. Ezekiel Ton, who is the most remarkable thing in poetry since Robert Browning. Mr. Ton, who has left America to reside for a while in London and impress his personality on English editors, publishers and readers, is by far the newest poet going, whatever other advertisements may say. He has succeeded, where all others have failed, in evolving a blend of the imagery of the unfettered West, the vocabulary of Wardour Street, and the sinister abandon of Borgiac Italy.

In 1913, someone writing to the New York *Nation* from the University of Illinois, illustrates the American, more serious, disapproval. This writer begins by expressing his objections to the "principle of Futurism." (Pound has perhaps done more than anyone to keep Futurism out of England. His antagonism to this movement was the first which was not due merely to unintelligent dislike for anything new, and was due to his perception that Futurism was incompatible with any principles of form. In his own words, Futurism is "accelerated impressionism.") The writer in the *Nation* then goes on to analyze the modern "hypertrophy of romanticism" into

> The exaggeration of the importance of a personal emotion.
> The abandonment of all standards of form.
> The suppression of all evidence that a particular composition is animated by any directing intelligence.

As for the first point, here are Mr. Pound's words in answer to the question, "do you agree that the great poet is never emotional?"

> Yes, absolutely; if by emotion is meant that he is at the mercy of every passing mood.... The only kind of emotion worthy of a poet is the inspirational emotion which energises and strengthens, and which is very remote from the everyday emotion of sloppiness and sentiment....

And as for the platform of Imagism, here are a few of Pound's "Don'ts for Imagists":

> Pay no attention to the criticisms of men who have never themselves written a notable work.
>
> Use no superfluous word and no adjective which does not reveal something.

> Go in fear of abstractions. Don't retail in mediocre verse what has already been done in good prose.
>
> Don't imagine that the art of poetry is any simpler than the art of music or that you can please the expert before you have spent at least as much effort on the art of verse as the average piano teacher spends on the art of music.
>
> Be influenced by as many great artists as you can, but have the decency either to acknowledge the debt outright or try to conceal it.
>
> Consider the definiteness of Dante's presentation as compared with Milton's. Read as much of Wordsworth as does not seem to be unutterably dull.
>
> If you want the gist of the matter go to Sappho, Catullus, Villon when he is in the vein, Gautier when he is not too frigid, or if you have not the tongues seek out the leisurely Chaucer.
>
> Good prose will do you no harm. There is good discipline to be had by trying to write it. Translation is also good training.

The emphasis here is certainly on discipline and form. The Chicago *Tribune* recognized this as "sound sense," adding:

> If this is Imagism ... we are for establishing Imagism by constitutional amendment and imprisoning without recourse to

> ink or paper all "literary" ladies or gents who break any of these canons.

But other reviewers were less approving. While the writer in the *Nation*, quoted above, dreads the anarchy impending, Mr. William Archer was terrified at the prospect of hieratic formalisation. Mr. Archer believes in the simple untaught muse:

> Mr. Pound's commandments tend too much to make of poetry a learned, self-conscious craft, to be cultivated by a guild of adepts, from whose austere laboratories spontaneity and simplicity are excluded.... A great deal of the best poetry in the world has very little technical study behind it.... There are scores and hundreds of people in England who could write this simple metre (i.e. of "A Shropshire Lad") successfully.

To be hanged for a cat and drowned for a rat is, perhaps, sufficient exculpation.

Probably Mr. Pound has won odium not so much by his theories as by his unstinted praise of certain contemporary authors whose work he has liked. Such expressions of approval are usually taken as a grievance—much more so than any personal abuse, which is comparatively a compliment—by the writers who escape his mention. He does not say "A., B., and C. are bad poets or novelists," but when he says "The work of X., Y., and Z. is in such and such respects the most important work in verse (or prose) since so and so," then A., B., and C. are aggrieved. Also, Pound has frequently expressed disapproval of Milton and Wordsworth.

After "Ripostes," Mr. Pound's idiom has advanced still farther. Inasmuch as "Cathay," the volume of translations from the Chinese, appeared prior to "Lustra," it is sometimes thought that his newer idiom is due to the Chinese influence. This is almost the reverse of the truth. The late Ernest Fenollosa left a quantity of manuscripts, including a great number of rough translations (literally exact) from the Chinese. After certain poems subsequently incorporated in "Lustra" had appeared in "Poetry," Mrs. Fenollosa recognized that in Pound the Chinese manuscripts would find the interpreter whom her husband would have wished; she accordingly forwarded the papers for him to do as he liked with. It is thus due to Mrs. Fenollosa's acumen that we have "Cathay"; it is not as a consequence of "Cathay" that we have "Lustra." This fact must be borne in mind.

Poems afterward embodied in "Lustra" appeared in "Poetry," in April, 1913, under the title of "Contemporanea." They included among others "Tenzone," "The Condolence," "The Garret," "Salutation the Second," and "Dance Figure."

There are influences, but deviously. It is rather a gradual development of experience into which literary experiences have entered. These have not brought the bondage of temporary enthusiasms, but have liberated the poet from his former restricted sphere. There is Catullus and Martial, Gautier, Laforgue and Tristan Corbière. Whitman is certainly not an influence; there is not a trace of him anywhere; Whitman and Mr. Pound are antipodean to each other. Of "Contemporanea" the *Chicago Evening Post* discriminatingly observed:

> Your poems in the April *Poetry* are so mockingly, so delicately, so unblushingly beautiful that you seem to have brought back into the world a grace which (probably) never existed, but which we discover by an imaginative process in Horace and Catullus.

It was a true insight to ally Pound to the Latin, not to the Greek poets.

Certain of the poems in "Lustra" have offended admirers of the verse of the "Personae" period. When a poet alters or develops, many of his admirers are sure to drop off. Any poet, if he is to survive as a writer beyond his twenty-fifth year, must alter; he must seek new literary influences; he will have different emotions to express. This is disconcerting to that public which likes a poet to spin his whole work out of the feelings of his youth; which likes to be able to open a new volume of his poems with the assurance that they will be able to approach it exactly as they approached the preceding. They do not like that constant readjustment which the following of Mr. Pound's work demands. Thus has "Lustra" been a disappointment to some; though it manifests no falling off in technique, and no impoverishment of feeling. Some of the poems (including several of the "Contemporanea") are a more direct statement of views than Pound's verse had ever given before. Of these poems, M. Jean de Bosschère writes:

> Everywhere his poems incite man to exist, to profess a becoming egotism, without which there can be no real altruism.
>
> I beseech you enter your life.
> I beseech you learn to say "I"
> When I question you.
> For you are no part, but a whole;
> No portion, but a being.
>
> ... One must be capable of reacting to stimuli for a moment,
> as a real, live person, even in face of as much of one's own
> powers as are arrayed against one;... The virile complaint,
> the revolt of the poet, all which shows his emotion,—that

is poetry.

> Speak against unconscious oppression,
> Speak against the tyranny of the unimaginative,
> Speak against bonds.
>
> Be against all forms of oppression,
> Go out and defy opinion.

This is the old cry of the poet, but more precise, as an expression of frank disgust:

> Go to the adolescent who are smothered in family.
> O, how hideous it is
> To see three generations of one house gathered together!
> It is like an old tree without shoots,
> And with some branches rotted and falling.

Each poem holds out these cries of revolt or disgust, but they are the result of his still hoping and feeling:

Let us take arms against this sea of stupidities. Pound ...has experience of the folly of the Philistines who read his verse. Real pain is born of this stupid interpretation, and one does not realize how deep it is unless one can feel, through the ejaculations and the laughter, what has caused these wounds, which are made deeper by what he knows, and what he has lost....

The tone, which is at once jocund and keen, is one of Pound's qualities. Ovid, Catullus—he does not disown them.

He only uses these accents for his familiars; with the others he is on the edge of paradox, pamphleteering, indeed of abuse....

This is the proper approach to the poems at the beginning of "Lustra," and to the short epigrams, which some readers find "pointless," or certainly "not poetry." They should read, then, the "Dance Figure," or "Near Périgord," and remember that all these poems come out of the same man.

Thine arms are as a young sapling under the bark;
Thy face as a river with lights.

White as an almond are thy shoulders;
As new almonds stripped from the husk.

Or the ending of "Near Périgord":

Bewildering spring, and by the Auvezère
Poppies and day's-eyes in the green émail
Rose over us; and we knew all that stream,
And our two horses had traced out the valleys;
Knew the low flooded lands squared out with poplars,
In the young days when the deep sky befriended.
And great wings beat above us in the twilight,
And the great wheels in heaven
Bore us together ... surging ... and apart ...
Believing we should meet with lips and hands ...

There shut up in his castle, Tairiran's,
She who had nor ears nor tongue save in her hands,
Gone, ah, gone—untouched, unreachable!
She who could never live save through one person,
She who could never speak save to one person,
And all the rest of her a shifting change,
A broken bundle of mirrors...!

Then turn at once to "To a Friend Writing on Cabaret Dancers."

It is easy to say that the language of "Cathay" is due to the Chinese. If one looks carefully at (1) Pound's other verse, (2) other people's translations from the Chinese (e.g., Giles's), it is evident that this is not the case. The language was ready for the Chinese poetry. Compare, for instance, a passage from "Provincia Deserta":

I have walked
        into Périgord
I have seen the torch-flames, high-leaping,
Painting the front of that church,—
And, under the dark, whirling laughter,
I have looked back over the stream
        and seen the high building,
Seen the long minarets, the white shafts.
I have gone in Ribeyrac,
        and in Sarlat.
I have climbed rickety stairs, heard talk of Croy,
Walked over En Bertran's old layout,
Have seen Narbonne, and Cahors and Chalus,
Have seen Excideuil, carefully fashioned.

with a passage from "The River Song":

He goes out to Hori, to look at the wing-flapping storks,
He returns by way of Sei rock, to hear the new nightingales,
For the gardens at Jo-run are full of new nightingales,
Their sound is mixed in this flute,
Their voice is in the twelve pipes here.

It matters very little how much is due to Rihaku and how much to Pound. Mr. Ford Madox Hueffer has observed: "If these are original verses, then Mr. Pound is the greatest poet of this day." He goes on to say:

> The poems in "Cathay" are things of a supreme beauty. What poetry should be, that they are. And if a new breath of imagery and handling can do anything for our poetry, that new breath these poems bring....
>
> Poetry consists in so rendering concrete objects that the emotions produced by the objects shall arise in the reader....
>
> Where have you better rendered, or more permanently beautiful a rendering of, the feelings of one of those lonely watchers, in the outposts of progress, whether it be Ovid in Hyrcania, a Roman sentinel upon the great wall of this country, or merely ourselves, in the lonely recesses of our minds, than the "Lament of the Frontier Guard"?...
>
> Beauty is a very valuable thing; perhaps it is the most valuable thing in life; but the power to express emotion so that it shall communicate itself intact and exactly is almost more valuable. Of both these qualities Mr. Pound's book is very full. Therefore, I think we may say that this is much the best work he has done, for, however closely he may have followed his originals—and of that most of us have no means of judging—there is certainly a good deal of Mr. Pound in this little volume.

"Cathay" and "Lustra" were followed by the translations of Noh plays. The Noh are not so important as the Chinese poems (certainly not so important for English); the attitude is less unusual to us; the work is not so solid, so firm. "Cathay" will, I believe, rank with the "Sea-Farer" in the future among Mr. Pound's original work; the Noh will rank among his translations. It is rather a dessert after "Cathay." There are, however, passages which, as Pound has handled them, are different both from the Chinese and from anything existent in English. There is, for example, the fine speech of the old Kagekiyo, as he thinks of his youthful valour:

> He thought, how easy this killing. He rushed with his spearshaft gripped under his arm. He cried out, "I am Kagekiyo of the Heike." He rushed on to take them. He pierced through the helmet vizards of Miyanoya. Miyanoya fled twice, and again; and Kagekiyo cried: "You shall not escape me!" He leaped and wrenched off his helmet. "Eya!" The vizard broke and remained in his hand, and Miyanoya still fled afar, and afar, and he looked back crying in terror, "How terrible, how heavy your arm!" And Kagekiyo called at him, "How tough the shaft of your neck is!" And they both laughed out over the battle, and went off each his own way.

The "Times Literary Supplement" spoke of Mr. Pound's "mastery of beautiful diction" and his "cunningly rhythmically prose," in its review of the "Noh."

Even since "Lustra," Mr. Pound has moved again. This move is to the epic, of which three cantos appear in the American "Lustra" (they have already appeared in "Poetry"—Miss Monroe deserves great honour for her courage in printing an epic poem in this twentieth century—but the version in "Lustra" is revised and is improved by revision). We will leave it as a test: when anyone has studied Mr. Pound's poems in *chronological* order, and has mastered "Lustra" and "Cathay," he is prepared for the Cantos— but not till then. If the reader then fails to like them, he has probably omitted some step in his progress, and had better go back and retrace the journey.

Tradition and the Individual Talent

I

In English writing we seldom speak of tradition, though we occasionally apply its name in deploring its absence. We cannot refer to "the tradition" or to "a tradition"; at most, we employ the adjective in saying that the poetry of So-and-so is "traditional" or even "too traditional." Seldom, perhaps, does the word appear except in a phrase of censure. If otherwise, it is vaguely approbative, with the implication, as to the work approved, of some pleasing archæological reconstruction. You can hardly make the word agreeable to English ears without this comfortable reference to the reassuring science of archæology.

Certainly the word is not likely to appear in our appreciations of living or dead writers. Every nation, every race, has not only its own creative, but its own critical turn of mind; and is even more oblivious of the shortcomings and limitations of its critical habits than of those of its creative genius. We know, or think we know, from the enormous mass of critical writing that has appeared in the French language the critical method or habit of the French; we only conclude (we are such unconscious people) that the French are "more critical" than we, and sometimes even plume ourselves a little with the fact, as if the French were the less spontaneous. Perhaps they are; but we might remind ourselves that criticism is as inevitable as breathing, and that we should be none the worse for articulating what passes in our minds when we read a book and feel an emotion about it, for criticizing our own minds in their work of criticism. One of the facts that might come to light in this process is our tendency to insist, when we praise a poet, upon those aspects of his work in which he least resembles anyone else. In these aspects or parts of his work we pretend to find what is individual, what is the peculiar essence of the man. We dwell with satisfaction upon the poet's difference from his predecessors, especially his immediate predecessors; we endeavour to find something that can be isolated in order to be enjoyed. Whereas if we approach a poet without this prejudice we shall often find that not only the best, but the most individual parts of his work may be those in which the dead poets, his ancestors, assert their immortality most vigorously. And I do not mean the impressionable period of adolescence, but the period of full maturity.

Yet if the only form of tradition, of handing down, consisted in following the ways of the immediate generation before us in a blind or timid adherence to its successes, "tradition" should positively be discouraged. We have seen many such simple currents soon lost in the sand; and novelty is better than repetition. Tradition is a matter of much wider significance. It cannot be inherited, and if you want it you must obtain it by great labour. It involves, in the first place, the historical sense, which we may call nearly indispensable to anyone who would continue to be a poet beyond his twenty-fifth year; and the historical sense involves a perception, not only of the pastness of the past, but of its presence; the historical sense compels a man to write not merely with his own generation in his bones, but with a feeling that the whole of the literature of Europe from Homer and within it the whole of the literature of his own country has a simultaneous existence and composes a simultaneous order. This historical sense, which is a sense of the timeless as well as of the temporal and of the timeless and of the temporal together, is what makes a writer traditional. And it is at the same time what makes a writer most acutely conscious of his place in time, of his contemporaneity.

No poet, no artist of any art, has his complete meaning alone. His significance, his appreciation is the appreciation of his relation to the dead poets and artists. You cannot value him alone; you must set him, for contrast and comparison, among the dead. I mean this as a principle of æsthetic, not merely historical, criticism. The necessity that he shall conform, that he shall cohere, is not one-sided; what happens when a new work of art is created is something that happens simultaneously to all the works of art which preceded it. The existing monuments form an ideal order among themselves, which is modified by the introduction of the new (the really new) work of art among them. The existing order is complete before the new work arrives; for order to persist after the supervention of novelty, the *whole* existing order must be, if ever so slightly, altered; and so the relations, proportions, values of each work of art toward the whole are readjusted; and this is conformity between the old and the new. Whoever has approved this idea of order, of the form of European, of English literature, will not find it preposterous that the past should be altered by the present as much as the present is directed by the past. And the poet who is aware of this will be aware of great difficulties and responsibilities.

In a peculiar sense he will be aware also that he must inevitably be judged by the standards of the past. I say judged, not amputated, by them; not judged to be as good as, or worse or better than, the dead; and certainly not judged by the canons of dead critics. It is a judgment, a comparison, in which two things are measured by each other. To conform merely would be for the new work not really to conform at all; it would not be new, and would therefore not be a work of art. And we do not quite say that the new is more valuable because it fits in; but its fitting in is a test of its value—a test, it is true, which can only be slowly and cautiously applied, for we are none of us infallible judges of conformity. We say: it appears to conform, and is perhaps individual, or it appears individual, and may conform; but we are hardly likely to find that it is one and not the other.

To proceed to a more intelligible exposition of the relation of the poet to the past: he can neither take the past as a lump, an indiscriminate bolus, nor can he form himself wholly on one or two private admirations, nor can he form himself wholly upon one preferred period. The first course is inadmissible, the second is an important experience of youth, and the third is a pleasant and highly desirable supplement. The poet must be very conscious of the main current, which does not at all flow invariably through the most distinguished reputations. He must be quite aware of the obvious fact that art never improves, but that the material of art is never quite the same. He must be aware that the mind of Europe—the mind of his own country—a mind which he learns in time to be much more important than his own private mind—is a mind which changes, and that this change is a development which abandons nothing *en route*, which does not superannuate either Shakespeare, or Homer, or the rock drawing of the Magdalenian draughtsmen. That this development, refinement perhaps, complication certainly, is not, from the point of view of the artist, any improvement. Perhaps not even an improvement from the point of view of the psychologist or not to the extent which we imagine; perhaps only in the end based upon a complication in economics and machinery. But the difference between the present and the past is that the conscious present is an awareness of the past in a way and to an extent which the past's awareness of itself cannot show.

Some one said: "The dead writers are remote from us because we *know* so much more than they did." Precisely, and they are that which we know.

I am alive to a usual objection to what is clearly part of my programme for the *métier* of poetry. The objection is that the doctrine requires a ridiculous amount of erudition (pedantry), a claim which can be rejected by appeal to the lives of poets in any pantheon. It will even be affirmed that much learning deadens or perverts poetic sensibility. While, however, we persist in believing that a poet ought to know as much as will not encroach upon his necessary receptivity and necessary laziness, it is not desirable to confine knowledge to whatever can be put into a useful shape for examinations, drawing-rooms, or the still more pretentious modes of publicity. Some can absorb knowledge, the more tardy must sweat for it. Shakespeare acquired more essential history from Plutarch than most men could from the whole British Museum. What is to be insisted upon is that the poet must develop or procure the consciousness of the past and that he should continue to develop this consciousness throughout his career.

What happens is a continual surrender of himself as he is at the moment to something which is more valuable. The progress of an artist is a continual self-sacrifice, a continual extinction of personality.

There remains to define this process of depersonalization and its relation to the sense of tradition. It is in this depersonalization that art may be said to approach the condition of science. I shall, therefore, invite you to consider, as a suggestive analogy, the action which takes place when a bit of finely filiated platinum is introduced into a chamber containing oxygen and sulphur dioxide.

II

Honest criticism and sensitive appreciation is directed not upon the poet but upon the poetry. If we attend to the confused cries of the newspaper critics and the susurrus of popular repetition that follows, we shall hear the names of poets in great numbers; if we seek not Blue-book knowledge but the enjoyment of poetry, and ask for a poem, we shall seldom find it. In the last article I tried to point out the importance of the relation of the poem to other poems by other authors, and suggested the conception of poetry as a living whole of all the poetry that has ever been written. The other aspect of this Impersonal theory of poetry is the relation of the poem to its author. And I hinted, by an analogy, that the mind of the mature poet differs from that of the immature one not precisely in any valuation of "personality," not being necessarily more interesting, or having "more to say," but rather by being a more finely perfected medium in which special, or very varied, feelings are at liberty to enter into new combinations.

The analogy was that of the catalyst. When the two gases previously mentioned are mixed in the presence of a filament of platinum, they form sulphurous acid. This combination takes place only if the platinum is present; nevertheless the newly formed acid contains no trace of platinum, and the platinum itself is apparently unaffected; has remained inert, neutral, and unchanged. The mind of the poet is the shred of platinum. It may partly or exclusively operate upon the experience of the man himself; but, the more perfect the artist, the more completely separate in him will be the man who suffers and the mind which creates; the more perfectly will the mind digest and transmute the passions which are its material.

The experience, you will notice, the elements which enter the presence of the transforming catalyst, are of two kinds: emotions and feelings. The effect of a work of art upon the person who enjoys it is an experience different in kind from any experience not of art. It may be formed out of one emotion, or may be a combination of several; and various feelings, inhering for the writer in particular words or phrases or images, may be added to compose the final result. Or great poetry may be made without the direct use of any emotion whatever: composed out of feelings solely. Canto XV of the *Inferno* (Brunetto Latini) is a working up of the emotion evident in the situation; but the effect, though single as that of any work of art, is obtained by considerable complexity of detail. The last quatrain gives an image, a feeling attaching to an image, which "came," which did not develop simply out of what precedes, but which was probably in suspension in the poet's mind until the proper combination arrived for it to add itself to. The poet's mind is in fact a receptacle for seizing and storing up numberless feelings, phrases, images, which remain there until all the particles which can unite to form a new compound are present together.

If you compare several representative passages of the greatest poetry you see how great is the variety of types of combination, and also how completely any semi-ethical criterion of "sublimity" misses the mark. For it is not the "greatness," the intensity, of the emotions, the components, but the intensity of the artistic process, the pressure, so to speak, under which the fusion takes place, that counts. The episode of Paolo and Francesca employs a definite emotion, but the intensity of the poetry is something quite different from whatever intensity in the supposed experience it may give the impression of. It is no more intense, furthermore, than Canto XXVI, the voyage of Ulysses, which has not the direct dependence upon an emotion. Great variety is possible in the process of transmution of emotion: the murder of Agamemnon, or the agony of Othello, gives an artistic effect apparently closer to a possible original than the scenes from Dante. In the *Agamemnon*, the artistic emotion approximates to the emotion of an actual spectator; in *Othello* to the emotion of the protagonist himself. But the difference between art and the event is always absolute; the combination which is the murder of Agamemnon is probably as complex as that which is the voyage of Ulysses. In either case there has been a fusion of elements. The ode of Keats contains a number of feelings which have nothing particular to do with the nightingale, but which the nightingale, partly, perhaps, because of its attractive name, and partly because of its reputation, served to bring together.

The point of view which I am struggling to attack is perhaps related to the metaphysical theory of the substantial unity of the soul: for my meaning is, that the poet has, not a "personality" to express, but a particular medium, which is only a medium and not a personality, in which impressions and experiences combine in peculiar and unexpected ways. Impressions and experiences which are important for the man may take no place in the poetry, and those which become important in the poetry may play quite a negligible part in the man, the personality.

I will quote a passage which is unfamiliar enough to be regarded with fresh attention in the light—or darkness—of these observations:

And now methinks I could e'en chide myself
For doating on her beauty, though her death
Shall be revenged after no common action.
Does the silkworm expend her yellow labours
For thee? For thee does she undo herself?
Are lordships sold to maintain ladyships
For the poor benefit of a bewildering minute?
Why does yon fellow falsify highways,
And put his life between the judge's lips,
To refine such a thing—keeps horse and men
To beat their valours for her?...

In this passage (as is evident if it is taken in its context) there is a combination of positive and negative emotions: an intensely strong attraction toward beauty and an equally intense fascination by the ugliness which is contrasted with it and which destroys it. This balance of contrasted emotion is in the dramatic situation to which the speech is pertinent, but that situation alone is inadequate to it. This is, so to speak, the structural emotion, provided by the drama. But the whole effect, the dominant tone, is due to the fact that a number of floating feelings, having an affinity to this emotion by no means superficially evident, have combined with it to give us a new art emotion.

It is not in his personal emotions, the emotions provoked by particular events in his life, that the poet is in any way remarkable or interesting. His particular emotions may be simple, or crude, or flat. The emotion in his poetry will be a very complex thing, but not with the complexity of the emotions of people who have very complex or unusual emotions in life. One error, in fact, of eccentricity in poetry is to seek for new human emotions to express; and in this search for novelty in the wrong place it discovers the perverse. The business of the poet is not to find new emotions, but to use the ordinary ones and, in working them up into poetry, to express feelings which are not in actual emotions at all. And emotions which he has never experienced will serve his turn as well as those familiar to him. Consequently, we must believe that "emotion recollected in tranquillity" is an inexact formula. For it is neither emotion, nor recollection, nor, without distortion of meaning, tranquillity. It is a concentration, and a new thing resulting from the concentration, of a very great number of experiences which to the practical and active person would not seem to be experiences at all; it is a concentration which does not happen consciously or of deliberation. These experiences are not "recollected," and they finally unite in an atmosphere which is "tranquil" only in that it is a passive attending upon the event. Of course this is not quite the whole story. There is a great deal, in the writing of poetry, which must be conscious and deliberate. In fact, the bad poet is usually unconscious where he ought to be conscious, and conscious where he ought to be unconscious. Both errors tend to make him "personal." Poetry is not a turning loose of emotion, but an escape from emotion; it is not the expression of personality, but an escape from personality. But, of course, only those who have personality and emotions know what it means to want to escape from these things.

III

ὁ δὲ νοῦς ἴσως θειότερόν τι καὶ ἀπαθές ἐστιν

This essay proposes to halt at the frontier of metaphysics or mysticism, and confine itself to such practical conclusions as can be applied by the responsible person interested in poetry. To divert interest from the poet to the poetry is a laudable aim: for it would conduce to a juster estimation of actual poetry, good and bad. There are many people who appreciate the expression of sincere emotion in verse, and there is a smaller number of people who can appreciate technical excellence. But very few know when there is expression of *significant* emotion, emotion which has its life in the poem and not in the history of the poet. The emotion of art is impersonal. And the poet cannot reach this impersonality without surrendering himself wholly to the work to be done. And he is not likely to know what is to be done unless he lives in what is not merely the present, but the present moment of the past, unless he is conscious, not of what is dead, but of what is already living.

Hamlet and His Problems

FEW critics have even admitted that *Hamlet* the play is the primary problem, and Hamlet the character only secondary. And Hamlet the character has had an especial temptation for that most dangerous type of critic: the critic with a mind which is naturally of the creative order, but which through some weakness in creative power exercises itself in criticism instead. These minds often find in Hamlet a vicarious existence for their own artistic realization. Such a mind had Goethe, who made of Hamlet a Werther; and such had Coleridge, who made of Hamlet a Coleridge; and probably neither of these men in writing about Hamlet remembered that his first business was to study a work of art. The kind of criticism that Goethe and Coleridge produced, in writing of Hamlet, is the most misleading kind possible. For they both possessed unquestionable critical insight, and both make their critical aberrations the more plausible by the substitution—of their own Hamlet for Shakespeare's—which their creative gift effects. We should be thankful that Walter Pater did not fix his attention on this play.

Two recent writers, Mr. J. M. Robertson and Professor Stoll of the University of Minnesota, have issued small books which can be praised for moving in the other direction. Mr. Stoll performs a service in recalling to our attention the labours of the critics of the seventeenth and eighteenth centuries, observing that

> they knew less about psychology than more recent Hamlet critics, but they were nearer in spirit to Shakespeare's art; and as they insisted on the importance of the effect of the whole rather than on the importance of the leading character, they were nearer, in their old-fashioned way, to the secret of dramatic art in general.

Qua work of art, the work of art cannot be interpreted; there is nothing to interpret; we can only criticize it according to standards, in comparison to other works of art; and for "interpretation" the chief task is the presentation of relevant historical facts which the reader is not assumed to know. Mr. Robertson points out, very pertinently, how critics have failed in their "interpretation" of *Hamlet* by ignoring what ought to be very obvious: that *Hamlet* is a stratification, that it represents the efforts of a series of men, each making what he could out of the work of his predecessors. The *Hamlet* of Shakespeare will appear to us very differently if, instead of treating the whole action of the play as due to Shakespeare's design, we perceive his *Hamlet* to be superposed upon much cruder material which persists even in the final form.

We know that there was an older play by Thomas Kyd, that extraordinary dramatic (if not poetic) genius who was in all probability the author of two plays so dissimilar as the *Spanish Tragedy* and *Arden of Feversham;* and what this play was like we can guess from three clues: from the *Spanish Tragedy* itself, from the tale of Belleforest upon which Kyd's *Hamlet* must have been based, and from a version acted in Germany in Shakespeare's lifetime which bears strong evidence of having been adapted from the earlier, not from the later, play. From these three sources it is clear that in the earlier play the motive was a revenge-motive simply; that the action or delay is caused, as in the *Spanish Tragedy,* solely by the difficulty of assassinating a monarch surrounded by guards; and that the "madness" of Hamlet was feigned in order to escape suspicion, and successfully. In the final play of Shakespeare, on the other hand, there is a motive which is more important than that of revenge, and which explicitly "blunts" the latter; the delay in revenge is unexplained on grounds of necessity or expediency; and the effect of the "madness" is not to lull but to arouse the king's suspicion. The alteration is not complete enough, however, to be convincing. Furthermore, there are verbal parallels so close to the *Spanish Tragedy* as to leave no doubt that in places Shakespeare was merely *revising* the text of Kyd. And finally there are unexplained scenes—the Polonius-Laertes and the Polonius-Reynaldo scenes—for which there is little excuse; these scenes are not in the verse style of Kyd, and not beyond doubt in the style of Shakespeare. These Mr. Robertson believes to be scenes in the original play of Kyd reworked by a third hand, perhaps Chapman, before Shakespeare touched the play. And he concludes, with very strong show of reason, that the original play of Kyd was, like certain other revenge plays, in two parts of five acts each. The upshot of Mr. Robertson's examination is, we believe, irrefragable:

that Shakespeare's *Hamlet,* so far as it is Shakespeare's, is a play dealing with the effect of a mother's guilt upon her son, and that Shakespeare was unable to impose this motive successfully upon the "intractable" material of the old play.

Of the intractability there can be no doubt. So far from being Shakespeare's masterpiece, the play is most certainly an artistic failure. In several ways the play is puzzling, and disquieting as is none of the others. Of all the plays it is the longest and is possibly the one on which Shakespeare spent most pains; and yet he has left in it superfluous and inconsistent scenes which even hasty revision should have noticed. The versification is variable. Lines like

> Look, the morn, in russet mantle clad, Walks o'er the dew of yon high eastern hill,

are of the Shakespeare of *Romeo and Juliet.* The lines in Act v. sc. ii.,

> Sir, in my heart there was a kind of fighting That would not let me sleep... Up from my cabin, My sea-gown scarf'd about me, in the dark Grop'd I to find out them: had my desire; Finger'd their packet;

are of his quite mature. Both workmanship and thought are in an unstable condition. We are surely justified in attributing the play, with that other profoundly interesting play of "intractable" material and astonishing versification, *Measure for Measure,* to a period of crisis, after which follow the tragic successes which culminate in *Coriolanus. Coriolanus* may be not as "interesting" as *Hamlet,* but it is, with *Antony and Cleopatra,* Shakespeare's most assured artistic success. And probably more people have thought *Hamlet* a work of art because they found it interesting, than have found it interesting because it is a work of art. It is the "Mona Lisa" of literature.

The grounds of *Hamlet's* failure are not immediately obvious. Mr. Robertson is undoubtedly correct in concluding that the essential emotion of the play is the feeling of a son towards a guilty mother:

> [Hamlet's] tone is that of one who has suffered tortures on the score of his mother's degradation.... The guilt of a mother is an almost intolerable motive for drama, but it had to be maintained and emphasized to supply a psychological solution, or rather a hint of one.

This, however, is by no means the whole story. It is not merely the "guilt of a mother" that cannot be handled as Shakespeare handled the suspicion of Othello, the infatuation of Antony, or the pride of Coriolanus. The subject might conceivably have expanded into a tragedy like these, intelligible, self-complete, in the sunlight. *Hamlet,* like the sonnets, is full of some stuff that the writer could not drag to light, contemplate, or manipulate into art. And when we search for this feeling, we find it, as in the sonnets, very difficult to localize. You cannot point to it in the speeches; indeed, if you examine the two famous soliloquies you see the versification of Shakespeare, but a content which might be claimed by another, perhaps by the author of the *Revenge of Bussy d' Ambois,* Act v. sc. i. We find Shakespeare's *Hamlet* not in the action, not in any quotations that we might select, so much as in an unmistakable tone which is unmistakably not in the earlier play.

The only way of expressing emotion in the form of art is by finding an "objective correlative"; in other words, a set of objects, a situation, a chain of events which shall be the formula of that *particular* emotion; such that when the external facts, which must terminate in sensory experience, are given, the emotion is immediately evoked. If you examine any of Shakespeare's more successful tragedies, you will find this exact equivalence; you will find that the state of mind of Lady Macbeth walking in her sleep has been communicated to you by a skilful accumulation of imagined sensory impressions; the words of Macbeth on hearing of his wife's death strike us as if, given the sequence of events, these words were automatically released by the last event in the series. The artistic "inevitability" lies in this complete adequacy of the external to the emotion; and this is precisely what is deficient in *Hamlet.* Hamlet (the man) is dominated by an emotion which is inexpressible, because it is in *excess* of the facts as they appear. And the supposed identity of Hamlet with his author is genuine to this point: that Hamlet's bafflement at the absence of objective equivalent to his feelings is a prolongation of the bafflement of his creator in the face of his artistic problem. Hamlet is up against the difficulty that his disgust is occasioned by his mother, but that his mother is not an adequate equivalent for it; his disgust envelops and exceeds her. It is thus a feeling which he cannot understand; he cannot objectify it, and it therefore remains to poison life and obstruct action. None of the possible actions can satisfy it; and nothing that Shakespeare can do with the plot can express Hamlet for him. And it must be noticed that the very nature of the *données* of the problem precludes objective equivalence. To have heightened the criminality of Gertrude would have been to provide the formula for a totally different emotion in Hamlet; it is just *because* her character is so negative and insignificant that she arouses in Hamlet the feeling which she is incapable of representing.

The "madness" of Hamlet lay to Shakespeare's hand; in the earlier play a simple ruse, and to the end, we may presume, understood as a ruse by the audience. For Shakespeare it is less than madness and more than feigned. The levity of Hamlet, his repetition of phrase, his puns, are not part of a deliberate plan of dissimulation, but a form of emotional relief. In the character Hamlet it is the buffoonery of an emotion which can find no outlet in action; in the dramatist it is the buffoonery of an emotion which he cannot express in art. The intense feeling, ecstatic or terrible, without an object or exceeding its object, is something which every person of sensibility has known; it is doubtless a study to pathologists. It often occurs in adolescence: the ordinary person puts these feelings to sleep, or trims down his feeling to fit the business world; the artist keeps it alive by his ability to intensify the world to his emotions. The Hamlet of Laforgue is an adolescent; the Hamlet of Shakespeare is not, he has not that explanation and excuse. We must simply admit that here Shakespeare tackled a problem which proved too much for him. Why he attempted it at all is an insoluble puzzle; under compulsion of what experience he attempted to express the inexpressibly horrible, we cannot ever know. We need a great many facts in his biography; and we should like to know whether, and when, and after or at the same time as what personal experience, he read Montaigne, II. xii., *Apologie de Raimond Sebond.* We should have, finally, to know something which is by hypothesis unknowable, for we assume it to be an experience which, in the manner indicated, exceeded the facts. We should have to understand things which Shakespeare did not understand himself.

Dante

M. PAUL VALÉRY, a writer for whom I have considerable respect, has placed in his most recent statement upon poetry a paragraph which seems to me of very doubtful validity. I have not seen the complete essay, and know the quotation only as it appears in a critical notice in the *Athenæum*, July 23, 1920:

> *La philosophie, et même la morale tendirent à fuir les oeuvres pour se placer dans les réflexions qui les précèdent.... Parler aujourd'hui de poésie philosophique (fût-ce en invoquant Alfred de Vigny, Leconte de Lisle, et quelques autres), c'est naivement confondre des conditions et des applications de l'esprit incompatibles entre elles. N'est-ce pas oublier que le but de celui qui spécule est de fixer ou de créer une notion—c'est-à-dire un pouvoir et un instrument de pouvoir, cependant que le poète moderne essaie de produire en nous un état et de porter cet état exceptionnel au point d'une jouissance parfaite....*

It may be that I do M. Valéry an injustice which I must endeavour to repair when I have the pleasure of reading his article entire. But the paragraph gives the impression of more than one error of analysis. In the first place, it suggests that conditions have changed, that "philosophical" poetry may once have been permissible, but that (perhaps owing to the greater specialization of the modern world) it is now intolerable. We are forced to assume that what we do not like in our time was never good art, and that what appears to us good was always so. If any ancient "philosophical" poetry retains its value, a value which we fail to find in modern poetry of the same type, we investigate on the assumption that we shall find some difference to which the mere difference of date is irrelevant. But if it be maintained that the older poetry has a "philosophic" element and a "poetic" element which can be isolated, we have two tasks to perform. We must show first in a particular case—our case is Dante—that the philosophy is essential to the structure and that the structure is essential to the poetic beauty of the parts; and we must show that the philosophy is employed in a different form from that which it takes in admittedly unsuccessful philosophical poems. And if M. Valéry is in error in his complete exorcism of "philosophy," perhaps the basis of the error is his apparently commendatory interpretation of the effort of the modern poet, namely, that the latter endeavours "to produce in us a *state.*"

The early philosophical poets, Parmenides and Empedocles, were apparently persons of an impure philosophical inspiration. Neither their predecessors nor their successors expressed themselves in verse; Parmenides and Empedocles were persons who mingled with genuine philosophical ability a good deal of the emotion of the founder of a second-rate religious system. They were not interested exclusively in philosophy, or religion, or poetry, but in something which was a mixture of all three; hence their reputation as poets is low and as philosophers should be considerably below Heraclitus, Zeno, Anaxagoras, or Democritus. The poem of Lucretius is quite a different matter. For Lucretius was undoubtedly a poet. He endeavours to expound a philosophical system, but with a different motive from Parmenides or Empedocles, for this system is already in existence; he is really endeavouring to find the concrete poetic equivalent for this system —to find its complete equivalent in vision. Only, as he is an innovator in this art, he wavers between philosophical poetry and philosophy. So we find passages such as:

> But the velocity of thunderbolts is great and their stroke powerful, and they run through their course with a rapid descent, because the force when aroused first in all cases collects itself in the clouds and ... Let us now sing what causes the motion of the stars.... Of all these different smells then which strike the nostrils one may reach to a much greater distance than another....

2

But Lucretius' true tendency is to express an ordered vision of the life of man, with great vigour of real poetic image and often acute observation.

> *quod petiere, premunt arte faciuntque dolorem corporis et dentes inlidunt saepe labellis osculaque adfligunt, quia non est pura voluptas et stimuli subsunt qui instigant laedere id ipsum quodcumque est, rabies unde illaec germina surgunt... medio de fonte leoprum surgit amari aliquid quod in ipsis floribus angat... nec procumbere humi prostratum et pandere palmas ante deum delubra nec aras sanguine multo spargere quadrupedum nec votis nectere vota, sed mage pacata posse omnia mente tueri.*

The philosophy which Lucretius tackled was not rich enough in variety of feeling, applied itself to life too uniformly, to supply the material for a wholly successful poem. It was incapable of complete expansion into pure vision. But I must ask M. Valéry whether the "aim" of Lucretius' poem was "to fix or create a notion" or to fashion "an instrument of power."

Without doubt, the effort of the philosopher proper, the man who is trying to deal with ideas in themselves, and the effort of the poet, who may be trying to *realize* ideas, cannot be carried on at the same time. But this is not to deny that poetry can be in some sense philosophic. The poet can deal with philosophic ideas, not as matter for argument, but as matter for inspection. The original form of a philosophy cannot be poetic. But poetry can be penetrated by a philosophic idea, it can deal with this idea when it has reached the point of immediate acceptance, when it has become almost a physical modification. If we divorced poetry and philosophy altogether, we should bring a serious impeachment, not only against Dante, but against most of Dante's contemporaries.

Dante had the benefit of a mythology and a theology which had undergone a more complete absorption into life than those of Lucretius. It is curious that not only Dante's detractors, like the Petrarch of Landor's *Pentameron* (if we may apply so strong a word to so amiable a character), but some of his admirers, insist on the separation of Dante's "poetry" and Dante's "teaching." Sometimes the philosophy is confused with the allegory. The philosophy is an ingredient, it is a part of Dante's world just as it is a part of life; the allegory is the scaffold on which the poem is built. An American writer of a little primer of Dante, Mr. Henry Dwight Sidgwick, who desires to improve our understanding of Dante as a "spiritual leader," says:

> To Dante this literal Hell was a secondary matter; so it is to us. He and we are concerned with the allegory. That allegory is simple. Hell is the absence of God.... If the reader begins with the consciousness that he is reading about sin, spiritually understood, he never loses the thread, he is never at a loss, never slips back into the literal signification.

Without stopping to question Mr. Sidgwick on the difference between literal and spiritual sin, we may affirm that his remarks are misleading. Undoubtedly the allegory is to be taken seriously, and certainly the *Comedy* is in some way a "moral education." The question is to find a formula for the correspondence between the former and the latter, to decide whether the moral value corresponds directly to the allegory. We can easily ascertain what importance Dante assigned to allegorical method. In the *Convivio* we are seriously informed that

> the principal design [of the odes] is to lead men to knowledge and virtue, as will be seen in the progress of the truth of them;

and we are also given the familiar four interpretations of an ode: literal, allegorical, moral, and anagogical. And so distinguished a scholar as M. Hauvette repeats again and again the phrase "didactique d'intention." We accept the allegory. Accepted, there are two usual ways of dealing with it. One may, with Mr. Sidgwick, dwell upon its significance for the seeker of "spiritual light," or one may, with Landor, deplore the spiritual mechanics and find the poet only in passages where he frees himself from his divine purposes. With neither of these points of view can we concur. Mr. Sidgwick magnifies the "preacher and prophet," and presents Dante as a superior Isaiah or Carlyle; Landor reserves the poet, reprehends the scheme, and denounces the politics. Some of Landor's errors are more palpable than Mr. Sidgwick's. He errs, in the first place, in judging Dante by the standards of classical epic. Whatever the *Comedy* is, an epic it is not. M. Hauvette well says:

> *Rechercher dans quelle mesure le poème se rapproche du genre classique de l'épopée, et dans quelle mesure il s'en écarte, est un exércice de rhétorique entièrement inutile, puisque Dante, à n'en pas douter, n'a jamais eu l'intention de composer une action épique dans les règles.*

But we must define the framework of Dante's poem from the result as well as from the intention. The poem has not only a framework, but a form; and even if the framework be allegorical, the form may be something else. The examination of any episode in the *Comedy* ought to show that not merely the allegorical interpretation or the didactic intention, but the emotional significance itself, cannot be isolated from the rest of the poem. Landor appears, for instance, to have misunderstood such a passage as the Paolo and Francesca, by failing to perceive its relations:

> In the midst of her punishment, Francesca, when she comes to the tenderest part of her story, tells it with complacency and delight.

This is surely a false simplification. To have lost all recollected delight would have been, for Francesca, either loss of humanity or relief from damnation. The ecstasy, with the present thrill at the remembrance of it, is a part of the torture. Francesca is neither stupefied nor reformed; she is merely damned; and it is a part of damnation to experience desires that we can no longer gratify. For in Dante's Hell souls are not deadened, as they mostly are in life; they are actually in the greatest torment of which each is capable.

> *E il modo ancor m'offende.*

It is curious that Mr. Sidgwick, whose approbation is at the opposite pole from Landor's, should have fallen into a similar error. He says:

> In meeting [Ulysses], as in meeting Pier della Vigna and Brunetto Latini, the preacher and the prophet are lost in the poet.

Here, again, is a false simplification. These passages have no digressive beauty. The case of Brunetto is parallel to that of Francesca. The emotion of the passage resides in Brunetto's excellence in damnation—so admirable a soul, and so perverse.

e parve de costoro Quegli che vince e non colui che perde.

And I think that if Mr. Sidgwick had pondered the strange words of Ulysses,

com' altrui piacque,

he would not have said that the preacher and prophet are lost in the poet. "Preacher" and "prophet" are odious terms; but what Mr. Sidgwick designates by them is something which is certainly not "lost in the poet," but is part of the poet.

A variety of passages might illustrate the assertion that no emotion is contemplated by Dante purely in and for itself. The emotion of the person, or the emotion with which our attitude appropriately invests the person, is never lost or diminished, is always preserved entire, but is modified by the position assigned to the person in the eternal scheme, is coloured by the atmosphere of that person's residence in one of the three worlds. About none of Dante's character is there that ambiguity which affects Milton's Lucifer. The damned preserve any degree of beauty or grandeur that ever rightly pertained to them, and this intensifies and also justifies their damnation. As Jason

Guarda quel grande che viene! E per dolor non par lagrima spanda, Quanto aspetto reale ancor ritiene!

The crime of Bertrand becomes more lurid; the vindictive Adamo acquires greater ferocity, and the errors of Arnaut are corrected—

> Poi s'ascose nel foco che gli affina.

If the artistic emotion presented by any episode of the *Comedy* is dependent upon the whole, we may proceed to inquire what the whole scheme is. The usefulness of allegory and astronomy is obvious. A mechanical framework, in a poem of so vast an ambit, was a necessity. As the centre of gravity of emotions is more remote from a single human action, or a system of purely human actions, than in drama or epic, so the framework has to be more artificial and apparently more mechanical. It is not essential that the allegory or the almost unintelligible astronomy should be understood—only that its presence should be justified. The emotional structure within this scaffold is what must be understood—the structure made possible by the scaffold. This structure is an ordered scale of human emotions. Not, necessarily, *all* human emotions; and in any case all the emotions are limited, and also extended in significance by their place in the scheme.

But Dante's is the most comprehensive, the most ordered presentation of emotions that has ever been made. Dante's method of dealing with any emotion may be contrasted, not so appositely with that of other "epic" poets as with that of Shakespeare. Shakespeare takes a character apparently controlled by a simple emotion, and analyses the character and the emotion itself. The emotion is split up into constituents—and perhaps destroyed in the process. The mind of Shakespeare was one of the most *critical* that has ever existed. Dante, on the other hand, does not analyse the emotion so much as he exhibits its relation to other emotions. You cannot, that is, understand Dante's *Inferno* without the *Purgatorio* and the *Paradiso.* "Dante," says Landor's

Petrarch, "is the great master of the disgusting." That is true, though Sophocles at least once approaches him. But a disgust like Dante's is no hypertrophy of a single reaction: it is completed and explained only by the last canto of the *Paradiso.*

La forma universal di questo nodo, credo ch'io vidi,
perchè più di largo dicendo questo, mi sento ch'io godo.

The contemplation of the horrid or sordid or disgusting, by an artist, is the necessary and negative aspect of the impulse toward the pursuit of beauty. But not all succeed as did Dante in expressing the complete scale from negative to positive. The negative is the more importunate.

The structure of emotions, for which the allegory is the necessary scaffold, is complete from the most sensuous to the most intellectual and the most spiritual. Dante gives a concrete presentation of the most elusive:

Pareva a me che nube ne coprisse lucida, spessa, solida e
polita, quasi adamante che lo sol ferisse. Per entro sè
l'eterna margarita ne recepette, com' acqua recepe raggio
di luce, permanendo unita.

or

Nel suo aspetto tal dentro mi fei, qual si fe' Glauco nel
gustar dell' erba, che il fe' consorto in mar degli altri dei.

Again, in the *Purgatorio,* for instance in Canto XVI and Canto XVIII, occur passages of pure exposition of philosophy, the philosophy of Aristotle strained through the schools.

Lo natural e sempre senza errore, ma l' altro puote errar
per malo obbietto, o per poco o per troppo di vigore...

We are not here studying the philosophy, we *see* it, as part of the ordered world. The aim of the poet is to state a vision, and no vision of life can be complete which does not include the articulate formulation of life which human minds make.

Onde convenne legge per fren porre...

It is one of the greatest merits of Dante's poem that the vision is so nearly complete; it is evidence of this greatness that the significance of any single passage, of any of the passages that are selected as "poetry," is incomplete unless we ourselves apprehend the whole.

And Dante helps us to provide a criticism of M. Valéry's "modern poet" who attempts "to produce in us a *state.*" A state, in itself, is nothing whatever.

M. Valéry's account is quite in harmony with pragmatic doctrine, and with the tendencies of such a work as William James's *Varieties of Religious Experience.* The mystical experience is supposed to be valuable because it is a pleasant state of unique intensity. But the true mystic is not satisfied merely by feeling, he must pretend at least that he *sees,* and the absorption into the divine is only the necessary, if paradoxical, limit of this contemplation. The poet does not aim to excite—that is not even a test of his success—but to set something down; the state of the reader is merely that reader's particular mode of perceiving what the poet has caught in words. Dante, more than any other poet, has succeeded in dealing with his philosophy, not as a theory (in the modern and not the Greek sense of that word) or as his own comment or reflection, but in terms of something *perceived.* When most of our modern poets confine themselves to what they had perceived, they produce for us, usually, only odds and ends of still life and stage properties; but that does not imply so much that the method of Dante is obsolete, as that our vision is perhaps comparatively restricted.

NOTE.—My friend the Abbé Laban has reproached me for attributing to Landor, in this essay, sentiments which are merely the expression of his dramatic figure Petrarch, and which imply rather Landor's reproof of the limitations of the historical Petrarch's view of Dante, than the view of Landor himself. The reader should therefore observe this correction of my use of Landor's honoured name.

Jeremiah Webster earned a PhD in English from the University of Wisconsin-Milwaukee. His poetry and non-fiction have appeared in numerous journals including *North American Review, Crab Creek Review, Beloit Poetry Journal, The Midwest Quarterly, REAL, The Penwood Review, Euonia Review, Dappled Things, Rock and Sling,* and *Ruminate.* He teaches literature and writing at Northwest University in Kirkland, Washington.

www.ingramcontent.com/pod-product-compliance
Lightning Source LLC
LaVergne TN
LVHW010620100826
845148LV00014B/3051
* 9 7 8 0 6 1 5 9 1 4 6 2 6 *